MAXX CROSBY

BIOGRAPHY

The Relentless Raider Who Became One of the NFL's Most Dominant Defensive Forces

Robert N. Marsh

DISCLAIMER

This book is a biographical account of Maxx Crosby, based on thorough research, interviews, public records, and material available at the time of publication. Every effort has been made to ensure the accuracy of the information, though some details may be open to interpretation. Names, images, trademarks, and registered trademarks belong to their respective owners and are referenced only for clarity, with no intent to infringe upon their rights. This book is not officially endorsed by or associated with any organizations or governing bodies mentioned. The author and publisher are not responsible for any errors or omissions and will not be held legally accountable for any damages, losses, or financial implications resulting from the information provided, either directly or indirectly.

TABLE OF CONTENTS

INTRODUCTION

Maxx Crosby's journey from a small-town athlete to a celebrated NFL star is a remarkable testament to the power of determination, resilience, and relentless ambition. Born in the quaint town of Colleyville, Texas, Crosby's path was not without its hurdles, yet his unyielding spirit and passion for the game propelled him into the national spotlight. This book delves into the life of a player who has excelled on the field and has also become a symbol of perseverance and personal growth, inspiring countless individuals along the way.

From a young age, Maxx displayed an innate talent for football and an unshakeable drive to succeed. As he navigated the challenges of youth sports, his tenacity set him apart from his peers. While many athletes often face self-doubt or external pressures, Crosby's determination remained a guiding force. Each practice, each game, and each setback only fueled his desire to prove himself, not just to others but, most importantly, to himself. This fierce motivation laid the groundwork for what would become a remarkable career.

Crosby's collegiate career at Eastern Michigan University was a turning point. Here, he honed his skills, transforming raw talent into refined expertise. Despite skepticism from those who overlooked him due to his smaller stature than traditional NFL defensive linemen, Crosby thrived in an environment that encouraged hard work and dedication. His performance on the field garnered attention from scouts and solidified his identity as a player who could rise above expectations. The lessons learned during this time would serve him well as he transitioned into the highly competitive world of professional football.

When the NFL draft arrived, anticipation filled the air. Crosby's selection by the Las Vegas Raiders was a dream come true, marking the beginning of a new chapter in his life. However, the transition from college to the pros is fraught with challenges, and Crosby quickly realized that maintaining his performance in the NFL would require even greater effort and adaptation. It was a pivotal moment that tested his resolve and commitment to excellence. This book explores how Crosby navigated these challenges and emerged as a key figure in the Raiders' defensive lineup, known for his relentless pursuit of quarterbacks and unwavering commitment to his teammates.

Maxx Crosby's story is also one of vulnerability and redemption. Behind the bright lights and the accolades lies a journey marked by personal struggles, including battles with addiction and mental health. His willingness to confront these issues head-on and advocate for others in similar situations has transformed his life and made him a role model for many. His commitment to mental health awareness and addiction recovery is a testament to his character, illustrating that true strength comes from acknowledging one's weaknesses and seeking help.

As we explore the various chapters of Maxx's life, we will examine the key moments that shaped his career and the lessons he learned. From his early days in Texas to the bright lights of Las Vegas, each experience contributed to his development as a player and a person. We will delve into the aspects of his game that set him apart, his relentless work ethic, and his impact on his team and community.

This book is not just a chronicle of achievements; it explores what it means to strive for greatness in every aspect of life. Maxx Crosby's legacy extends beyond the football field, as he inspires others through advocacy and leadership. Readers will discover that his story is a powerful reminder of the importance of resilience, hard work, and overcoming adversity.

Through the lens of Maxx's experiences, we aim to highlight the transformative power of sport, the significance of community, and the indomitable human spirit. His journey reflects the essence of chasing one's dreams, facing challenges with courage, and emerging stronger on the other side. As we embark on this exploration of Maxx Crosby's life, we invite you to witness a story of ambition, growth, and unwavering commitment that resonates far beyond the boundaries of the football field.

Chapter 1: Early Life and Beginnings

Growing Up in Colleyville, Texas

Maxx Crosby's upbringing in Colleyville, Texas, significantly shaped the man and athlete he would become. Born and raised in a suburban town between Dallas and Fort Worth, Crosby was part of a tight-knit community where sports were essential to life. Colleyville is known for its strong support of high school athletics, and this environment naturally encouraged young Maxx to be active and competitive from an early age.

Growing up in a town like Colleyville, where families emphasized values like hard work and discipline, Maxx was surrounded by influences that pushed him toward achievement. His parents taught him the importance of working hard in the field and in life. They emphasized staying grounded and focused, two traits later defining him as an athlete. Family was central to his life, and his close bond with his parents and siblings gave him the stability and motivation to push forward, even when things got tough. His father, a strong figure, often reminded him that no success comes without sacrifice, and this principle became a core part of his mentality.

The streets and fields of Colleyville were familiar to him long before he gained national recognition. Whether playing neighborhood pick-up games with friends or participating in organized sports, Maxx found joy in competition. He was always eager to push himself on a local football field or during backyard games with other kids. As he grew older, it became clear that his physical gifts and work ethic set him apart from his peers. Yet, it wasn't just natural talent that marked him as special; he was determined to constantly improve and push past any limits others might have seen in him. While many kids his age enjoyed sports casually, Maxx took his passion for the game to another level, seeing every challenge as an opportunity to grow.

His passion for football grew alongside him, but it wasn't his only focus. In Colleyville, Maxx was involved in multiple activities, from school to other sports, learning valuable lessons. The multi-sport culture of the area meant that he tried his hand at everything from basketball to track and field, honing different aspects of his athleticism. The variety of experiences contributed to the well-rounded athletic skill set he would later bring to football. These formative years were crucial in developing the speed, agility, and physicality that would one day make him a feared defensive end.

At the heart of Crosby's journey was a love for football that developed early on. Watching games with his family became a regular tradition. The spectacle of the NFL, the intensity of high school matchups, and even collegiate competitions all ignited something within him. Like many young athletes, he dreamed of one day playing under the bright lights, competing at the highest levels, but it wasn't just about dreaming for him. Every weekend, he would see professionals on the television screen, and instead of being content as a spectator, he made a point to study their movements, discipline, and attitudes. He envisioned himself on that stage, not just as a fan but as a competitor. And while it was still a long way off, those early days of watching the game built the foundation for what would become his life's work.

Colleyville's competitive environment also meant that Maxx had plenty of local role models to look up to. From older high school athletes who went on to play in college to local sports figures, the town offered inspiration. His neighborhood was filled with stories of local heroes who made their way into various collegiate sports programs, and for a young Maxx, these stories planted a seed. Seeing others from his community succeed showed him that it was possible to turn ambition into reality. Maxx didn't just admire these athletes; he took mental notes on what it took to succeed.

However, Maxx wasn't just focused on sports. Growing up in a supportive household, academics were also a significant part of his upbringing. His parents ensured he understood the importance of balancing his athletic pursuits with schoolwork. Colleyville's schools were known for providing a robust academic environment, and Maxx was expected to meet the same standards as any other student. This helped him develop a sense of discipline that translated well into his football career. His parents instilled in him that hard work off the field was just as crucial as his effort during practices and games. These lessons of balancing responsibility would serve him well later on as he juggled the demands of being a high-profile athlete.

Even with his early passion for football, Maxx faced challenges growing up in Colleyville. As is common with many athletes, there were periods of self-doubt and obstacles to overcome. Whether struggling to master a technique or dealing with the physical toll that sports take on a young body, Maxx learned early on that nothing worth having comes easily. In moments of frustration, he could lean on his support system, particularly his parents, who constantly reinforced the belief that perseverance would lead to success. They reminded him that setbacks are part of the journey and encouraged him to view them as learning opportunities rather than reasons to quit.

As Maxx entered his teenage years, his dedication to football intensified. He started taking the game more seriously, and the results were clear. Coaches began to notice his abilities, not just as a naturally gifted athlete but as someone committed to improving every day. Whether showing up early for practice or staying late to work on his technique, Maxx displayed the work ethic that separates good players from great ones. His growth wasn't just physical; it was mental. He developed a toughness and resilience that would carry him through some of the more difficult periods of his athletic career.

Colleyville's local high school football scene was highly competitive, and Maxx thrived. The program he played for pushed athletes to excel, not just on game days but in every aspect of their preparation. Weight room sessions were intense, practices were physically demanding, and expectations were high. Maxx didn't shy away from these challenges; he embraced them. While some players might have been content to coast on natural ability, he made it clear to coaches and teammates that he was willing to work to be the best. The long hours of training, sweat, and grind became part of his identity as an athlete.

The values Maxx developed during his years in Colleyville would shape him long after he left the town. The discipline, work ethic, and sense of responsibility he absorbed as a young athlete set the stage for his future in the NFL. Even as he moved on to bigger stages and greater challenges, those early lessons stayed with him, reminding him of where he came from and the journey to reach the top. Colleyville may have been just one chapter in his story. Still, it was foundational, laying the groundwork for the success and perseverance defining Maxx Crosby's career as a dominant force in professional football.

The Influence of Family and Community

Maxx Crosby's rise to prominence as one of the NFL's top defensive players cannot be understood without recognizing the influence of his family and the surrounding community. His path to the professional level was shaped by the strong support system at home and the relationships and connections he built with those around him. This network provided the foundation for his success, encouraging him to chase his dreams and instilling the values that would guide him throughout his journey.

From an early age, Crosby's parents were central to his development. They encouraged him to be ambitious, instilling a sense of purpose that extended beyond sports. His mother and father were hands-on in his upbringing, ensuring he had the tools to succeed both on and off the field. They emphasized the importance of staying focused and working hard in life. Whether driving him to early morning practices or attending every game, their involvement was crucial to Maxx's growth. His parents were always present, not just as spectators but as active participants in his development. They offered the right balance of encouragement and discipline, never allowing him to settle for anything less than his best effort.

One of the most important lessons Maxx learned from his parents was the value of perseverance. No matter how difficult things became, his family taught him that setbacks were temporary and could be overcome with determination and hard work. This mindset was evident in his approach to football, where he frequently pushed himself beyond what was expected. His family created an environment where nothing was impossible, a message that stuck with him as he navigated the challenges of competitive sports. They instilled a belief that no matter the situation, giving up was never an option. That resilience, developed at home, would later serve him well during the more challenging periods of his career, particularly during his struggles with personal demons and the pressures of professional sports.

Maxx's father played a particularly significant role in his early football career. He wasn't just a supportive figure; he became a mentor in many ways. Having been involved in sports, his father understood the physical and mental demands of competition. He provided Maxx with insights into the mentality required to excel, reminding him that success wasn't just about talent but about preparation and mental fortitude. Whether offering advice after a tough game or helping Maxx fine-tune his approach, his father's presence helped shape the disciplined athlete Maxx would become. The lessons learned from his father were practical and grounded in real-world experience, and they stuck with Maxx as he moved through the ranks of high school and college football.

On the other hand, Maxx's mother brought balance to his upbringing. She emphasized the importance of maintaining a well-rounded life, encouraging Maxx to find joy outside of football. Her support was unwavering, whether through emotional encouragement or ensuring he stayed grounded. Maxx often credits his mother with helping him keep perspective, reminding him that football, while important, wasn't the entirety of his life. This grounded approach helped him navigate the highs and lows of a sports career. She was a constant presence, providing a listening ear and helping him maintain his confidence when things got tough. Maxx's relationship with his mother became a stabilizing force, particularly when the pressures of football threatened to overwhelm him.

Maxx also benefited from the influence of his older brother, who provided both a competitive spirit and a guiding hand. Sibling rivalry often fueled his desire to improve as he grew up trying to match his brother's accomplishments. Friendly competition between the two fostered a drive to succeed, pushing Maxx to constantly challenge himself. His brother wasn't just a rival but a role model who demonstrated the benefits of hard work and dedication. Watching his brother's journey in life gave Maxx a clear example of the rewards of staying disciplined and focused. They shared a bond that extended beyond sports, encouraging Maxx to strive for excellence in all areas of his life.

Beyond the family, Crosby's community played an equally important role in his development. Growing up in Colleyville, he was surrounded by people who supported his dreams and actively contributed to his success. The town had a rich tradition of high school athletics, with local teams regularly competing at a high level. Coaches, teachers, and local mentors provided guidance and opportunities that helped Maxx thrive. The community valued sportsmanship, and competition was a big part of local culture. As he became more involved in football, Maxx found himself surrounded by individuals who were just as invested in his growth as his family was. These local relationships helped him stay motivated and focused despite challenges.

His high school coaches, in particular, profoundly impacted his athletic and personal development. They taught him the technical aspects of football and stressed the importance of leadership and teamwork. They encouraged him to take on responsibility, pushing him to become a leader on the field. These early leadership lessons would become crucial as Maxx transitioned into the higher levels of competition. The structure provided by his high school coaches helped him develop a strong work ethic and an understanding of what it meant to be part of a team. The local football program wasn't just about winning games; it was about building character and fostering personal growth, and Maxx embraced these lessons wholeheartedly.

The support Maxx received from his peers and friends in the community also cannot be understated. Growing up in a close-knit environment, he was surrounded by friends who shared his love for football and understood the challenges of competitive sports. This network provided him with camaraderie, a place where he could relax and be himself, away from the pressures of the game. His friends were his biggest fans, attending games and celebrating his successes alongside him. This sense of belonging helped keep Maxx grounded, reminding him that his identity wasn't solely tied to his achievements on the football field.

As Maxx continued to rise through the ranks, his community's support grew stronger. By the time he reached college, he had become somewhat of a local hero, with people in Colleyville following his progress closely. They celebrated his victories and stood by him during tough times, always showing pride in what one of their own had accomplished. That sense of responsibility to his hometown fueled Maxx even more, as he recognized that his success wasn't just his own; it was shared by everyone who had supported him along the way. Whether it was the encouragement from old coaches, the messages of support from friends, or the pride of his family, Maxx knew that he wasn't walking the path alone.

The influence of both his family and community provided Maxx with a deep well of support, allowing him to stay focused and motivated even when the road became difficult. Their combined efforts gave him the tools to succeed as an athlete and a person. The values they instilled, hard work, perseverance, and humility, became the guiding principles that shaped his career. As he transitioned into the spotlight of professional football, those early lessons remained with him, providing the strength and stability needed to navigate the challenges of the NFL.

Maxx Crosby's success story is not just about individual talent or personal drive; it's a testament to the power of family and community. The support, guidance, and love he received from those around him played an integral role in his journey, reminding him that success is never achieved in isolation. Every step he took and every challenge he overcame was made possible by the foundation built by his family and community, which continues to support him as he reaches new heights in his career.

Discovering Football: The First Steps Toward Stardom

Maxx Crosby's introduction to football was a defining moment in his young life. While he grew up in a family that valued sports, his initial interest was not so much a calculated decision as it was a natural gravitation toward a game that captured his imagination. His early years were filled with typical childhood activities, but it wasn't until he stepped onto the football field that he discovered something different. Football gave him an outlet for his energy and competitive spirit, sparking a passion that would grow as he matured.

Maxx didn't immediately stand out as a star athlete in those early days. He was tall for his age but lacked the physicality many of his peers possessed. Yet, from the moment he picked up a football, it was clear that he loved the game. The first few seasons were more about learning the fundamentals than anything else. Like most young players, he developed basic skills like running, catching, and tackling. At first, there wasn't much pressure to succeed; it was about having fun and being part of a team. Those formative years allowed Maxx to explore the sport without the weight of expectations, which fostered his love for football even more.

His enthusiasm for the game deepened as he continued playing through his childhood. What started as a fun activity evolved into something he took seriously. He spent countless hours watching games, studying players, and dreaming of one day making an impact in football. The more he played, the more he recognized that he had potential, even if it wasn't immediately obvious. His coaches noticed his growing dedication and began investing more time in helping him develop his abilities. Maxx was known for his work ethic, even at a young age. He was never content with mediocrity and constantly sought to improve, whether staying late after practice or working on his technique at home.

One of the defining moments during Maxx's early football journey was when he began to understand the mental aspect of the game. Football was about strength or speed, strategy, discipline, and awareness. He started paying attention to details that others might overlook. While some kids his age were more focused on making flashy plays, Maxx was drawn to understanding the nuances of positioning, timing, and reading the game. His early interest in these finer details helped set him apart, giving him an edge as he progressed through different levels of competition.

However, football didn't come without its challenges. Maxx had his share of frustrations, particularly when his body hadn't yet caught up to his aspirations. He wasn't the biggest or the fastest, which sometimes seemed a disadvantage. Yet, rather than let those frustrations hold him back, Maxx used them as motivation. He knew that raw talent could only take a player so far and that hard work could close the gap between him and other athletes. So, he committed himself to outworking everyone else. He didn't shy away from tough practices or exhausting training sessions but embraced them. This dedication to improvement became one of the cornerstones of his journey toward football stardom.

Maxx's support from his coaches and teammates during those early years also played a pivotal role in his development. His coaches saw potential in him and pushed him to go beyond what he thought he was capable of. They recognized his strengths and helped him refine them while encouraging him to address areas where he could improve. His teammates, too, provided a sense of camaraderie and healthy competition. They challenged Maxx on the field, forcing him to raise his level of play to keep up. Being part of a team gave him a sense of purpose, teaching him the value of teamwork and collective effort, which would prove essential as he advanced in his football career.

As Maxx continued to grow and improve, he began to develop a style of play that would define him throughout his career. His position on the defensive line allowed him to channel his natural aggression and athleticism into a perfectly suited role. He excelled at getting to the quarterback and disrupting offensive plays. The more he played, the more comfortable he became in his role, and his confidence began to soar. The sense of satisfaction from making big plays, sacks, tackles for loss, and forced turnovers only fueled his drive further.

Another key factor in Maxx's early development was his ability to learn from setbacks. Like all athletes, he faced moments where things didn't go his way. Whether it was a tough loss or a poor performance, Maxx used those experiences as learning opportunities. He became adept at analyzing his mistakes and figuring out how to correct them. This ability to reflect and adapt became one of his greatest strengths. Rather than letting failure derail his progress, he embraced it as part of the journey. His resilience in the face of adversity was a trait that would later define his professional career, but its roots were established in these formative years.

The community around Maxx also provided a supportive environment for his growth. Football was more than just a sport in Colleyville; it was a cultural pillar. The local football programs were competitive, and the community took pride in developing young athletes. Maxx was surrounded by coaches, mentors, and peers who all shared a passion for the game. The town rallied around its young athletes, and Maxx benefited from that sense of belonging and support. Whether it was a local coach offering advice or a neighbor cheering him on during games, Maxx always felt like he had people rooting for him.

As Maxx entered his teenage years, his physical development began to catch up to his skills and work ethic. His body grew stronger, and he began to fill out his frame. His newfound physicality and sharp understanding of the game made him a formidable player. He started gaining attention from coaches and scouts, who recognized that he could play at higher levels. Yet, despite the attention, Maxx remained grounded. His focus was always on improving, not on the accolades. He understood that success in football wasn't given; it was earned through consistent effort and commitment.

Maxx's high school years transformed him from a passionate player into a standout athlete. His performances on the field became more dominant, and his leadership qualities started to emerge. Coaches relied on him to set the tone for the team regarding effort and attitude. He wasn't just playing for himself anymore but for his teammates, coaches, and community. This sense of responsibility added another layer of motivation for Maxx. He wanted to make those who had supported him proud, and that desire pushed him to work even harder.

The discovery of football was not just about finding a sport he loved; it was about finding a path to shape his future. Football became more than a hobby or a passion for Maxx; it became his identity. The early experiences, successes, and challenges laid the groundwork for what would eventually be a successful career at the collegiate and professional levels. The lessons he learned during those first years, hard work, perseverance, and resilience, would stay with him as he pursued his dreams of playing in the NFL.

Maxx Crosby never forgot those first steps as he moved forward in his career. They were the foundation upon which everything else was built, and they provided him with the tools he needed to overcome obstacles and rise to stardom. From the beginning, football was more than just a game for Maxx Crosby; it was the start of a journey that would take him to places he had only dreamed of. Those early days on the field were a testament to his determination and passion, which continue to define him as an athlete today.

Chapter 2: College Years at Eastern Michigan

Making a Name in College Football

Maxx Crosby's journey into college football began when he accepted a scholarship offer to play for Eastern Michigan University. The decision to attend a mid-major school rather than one of the larger, more prominent programs wasn't driven by a lack of ambition but rather a recognition of where he could make the most significant impact. He was determined to use this opportunity as a stepping stone, believing that success would come to those willing to work for it, no matter the platform.

His arrival at Eastern Michigan was the start of a transformative chapter. Crosby entered an environment where the competition was fierce, and every athlete vied to prove themselves. The shift from high school to college football required not only physical adjustments but also mental ones. The game's speed differed; the players were stronger and more skilled, and the expectations were higher. Maxx quickly understood that success in college football would take more than just raw talent; it would require an elevated level of commitment and focus.

Maxx's freshman season was a time for growth and learning. He redshirted that year, a common practice for young players adjusting to the collegiate level. Redshirting allowed him to observe, develop, and fine-tune his skills without the pressure of immediate game-time expectations. Though it meant sitting out official games, it allowed him to practice with the team, understand the playbook, and get a feel for the college football environment. Maxx used this time wisely, focusing on strength training, improving his technique, and absorbing as much as he could from the coaching staff and older players.

One of the key changes Maxx made during his first year was in his physical conditioning. College football demanded a level of fitness that went beyond anything he had experienced before. He knew he had to get bigger, stronger, and faster to compete at the collegiate level. Maxx spent countless hours in the weight room, pushing himself to improve his strength and endurance. The program at Eastern Michigan strongly emphasized physical conditioning, and Maxx embraced the challenge. His natural work ethic made him a standout, even during redshirt practices, where his dedication was impossible to ignore.

Once his redshirt year ended, Maxx was ready to make his mark on the field. He began his official college career in his sophomore year, where his hard work during the previous season quickly paid off. His impact on the defensive line was immediate. Playing defensive end, he brought an intensity that caught the attention of his coaches and opponents. Maxx was relentless in his pursuit of the ball, using his combination of speed, strength, and technique to disrupt plays and make life difficult for opposing quarterbacks. He quickly became one of the team's most consistent defensive players.

As his college career progressed, Maxx continued to build on his early successes. His sophomore season set the foundation for an impressive career, but he truly began to shine in his junior and senior years. During those seasons, Maxx became known for his ability to pressure the quarterback. His quickness off the line and his instinct for finding gaps in the offensive line made him a constant threat in the backfield. He was particularly adept at using his hands to fend off blockers, a skill he had honed through countless hours of practice.

Maxx's dedication to mastering his craft did not go unnoticed. By his junior year, he was a key player for Eastern Michigan and one of the top defensive linemen in the Mid-American Conference (MAC). He earned all-conference honors, a testament to his growing reputation. His ability to consistently perform at a high level against some of the best competition in the conference made him a player to watch. He became a cornerstone of Eastern Michigan's defense, and his performances helped elevate the team's overall standing in the MAC.

Despite his success, Maxx remained humble and focused on the bigger picture. He wasn't playing for personal accolades but to help his team win. That team-first mentality made him a leader on and off the field. His work ethic inspired his teammates, and his relentless attitude during games set the standard for the defense. Maxx led by example, whether staying late after practice to work on his technique or pushing himself to the limit during conditioning drills. His leadership qualities made him a star player and a respected figure in the locker room.

Off the field, Maxx also focused on his academics and personal development. He understood the importance of balancing football with his education and future aspirations. The support from the university and coaching staff helped him manage the demands of being a student-athlete, but his discipline allowed him to succeed. College provided him with opportunities to grow as a person, and he took full advantage of that. His experiences at Eastern Michigan shaped him both as a player and an individual, preparing him for the challenges after college.

One of the pivotal moments in Maxx's college career came when he realized that he had the potential to play at the professional level. His performances drew attention from NFL scouts, and there was talk about him being a possible draft pick. This was both exciting and daunting for Maxx. It validated all the hard work he had put in but added a new level of pressure. He knew that to make it to the NFL, he would have to continue pushing himself even harder. There was no room for complacency.

Maxx responded to this challenge by elevating his game during his senior year. He knew that scouts were watching and wanted to leave no doubt about his readiness for the next level. Some of his best performances marked his final season at Eastern Michigan. He finished the season with impressive stats, including many sacks and tackles for loss. His ability to disrupt offenses and create turnovers became his trademark, and he solidified his place as one of the top defensive players in the conference.

As Maxx's college career ended, he faced the difficult decision of whether to declare for the NFL Draft or return for another year. After careful consideration and with the support of his coaches and family, he chose to pursue his dream of playing professional football. It was a bittersweet moment, as he would be leaving behind the team and the university that had given him so much, but he knew it was the right time to take the next step. Maxx had accomplished everything he set out to do at Eastern Michigan, and now it was time to see if he could succeed at the sport's highest level.

Making a name in college football wasn't easy, but Maxx Crosby had done it through hard work, determination, and a relentless pursuit of improvement. His time at Eastern Michigan had been the proving ground where he refined his skills and developed the mentality to serve him well in the NFL. The lessons he learned in college about discipline, leadership, and perseverance were invaluable. Maxx's journey from a redshirt freshman to one of the top defensive players in the MAC was a testament to his ability to rise to the occasion, no matter his challenges.

Challenges and Breakthroughs on the Field

Throughout Maxx Crosby's collegiate career, he encountered challenges that tested his resolve and commitment to football. Each obstacle served as an opportunity for growth, shaping him not only as an athlete but also as a person. A steep learning curve marked the transition from high school to college football. The competition level was higher, and the physical demands were greater. The jump to college football can be overwhelming for many athletes, but

Maxx embraced these challenges as stepping stones toward his aspirations.

One of the most significant hurdles he faced was adjusting to the physicality of college-level play. Coming from a high school where he had been a dominant force, Maxx soon realized he was no longer the biggest or strongest player on the field. This newfound reality meant that he had to elevate his training regimen. He quickly adapted by focusing on strength and conditioning, spending countless hours in the gym, working on his agility, and honing his techniques. Maxx dedicated himself to pushing past his limits, knowing he could only keep pace with his peers through rigorous training.

Another challenge arose during his first season on the field. Inconsistencies in performance can plague even the most talented players. Early in his sophomore year, Maxx struggled to maintain the level of play that had characterized his practices. It was a difficult realization that even with all his hard work, there would be days when things did not go as planned. His coaches recognized the dip in his performance and emphasized the importance of mental toughness. They urged him to trust his instincts, remain confident, and remember the skills that had brought him success. This period of self-reflection became crucial in his development. Maxx learned to identify the mental barriers that sometimes hindered him and began to work on strengthening his mindset alongside his physical skills.

As the season progressed, Maxx encountered another setback: injuries. Injuries can strike at any time, and for athletes, they often feel like the ultimate betrayal. Midway through his junior year, he suffered a minor injury that sidelined him for a few games. The emotional toll was considerable. Watching from the sidelines, he experienced frustration and a sense of helplessness. However, this period of forced rest allowed him to reassess his approach to the game. Rather than allowing the injury to derail him, he used the time to study game film, learn from his teammates, and develop a deeper understanding of the strategic aspects of football. This period of analysis and observation proved invaluable, as it provided insights into his opponents and highlighted areas where he could further enhance his game.

Maxx's ability to overcome these challenges was not solely reliant on his determination. He found strength and encouragement from his coaches and teammates, who significantly influenced his growth. They provided support, guidance, and constructive feedback that helped him navigate tough moments. He began to view challenges as collaborative experiences rather than solitary battles. The Eastern Michigan football program culture emphasized teamwork, resilience, and a shared commitment to improvement. It was this environment that fostered Maxx's growth, allowing him to flourish both as an individual and as a member of the team.

Breakthrough moments punctuated Maxx's journey, transforming his perspective and elevating his performance. The first of these came during a critical matchup against a rival school. It was a defining game that could determine the team's trajectory for the season. Maxx felt the weight of expectations on his shoulders, both from himself and the coaching staff. Leading up to the game, he committed to rigorous preparation, focusing on his physical training and mental visualization techniques. This practice allowed him to mentally rehearse his plays and anticipate his opponents' movements.

When game day arrived, Maxx was ready to make an impact. He was in the zone as the game unfolded, demonstrating remarkable focus and energy. His performance was electric; he made crucial tackles, pressured the quarterback, and played with an intensity that impressed everyone. The cheers from the crowd only fueled his fire. This game became a turning point in his career, instilling a belief in his abilities and solidifying his reputation as a force on the field. The experience taught him the importance of preparation, confidence, and overcoming adversity to succeed.

The culmination of his efforts came during his senior season, where he was able to showcase his growth and determination. With the support of his coaches and teammates, Maxx began to play with a new level of confidence and consistency. His statistics improved significantly, with an impressive number of sacks and tackles for loss. Scouts and coaches recognized his relentless pursuit of excellence, earning him accolades reflecting his hard work and perseverance. Each tackle and sack became a testament to his commitment to overcoming challenges and making a name for himself.

Maxx also developed a keen understanding of the game. He began to study not just his plays but also the strategies of opposing teams. This analytical approach allowed him to anticipate their movements, leading to improved performance on the field. The knowledge he gained from watching films and studying opponents gave him an edge that set him apart from many of his peers. This transition from being a talented player to becoming a strategic thinker marked a significant breakthrough in his development.

As his college career neared its conclusion, Maxx faced the challenge of transitioning from college football to the professional level. The prospect of entering the NFL was both exciting and daunting. With his performances drawing attention, he knew the time had come to take the next step. The transition from collegiate play to the NFL is uncertain, and many athletes struggle with the adjustment. However, Maxx was equipped with the tools he needed to succeed. His experiences at Eastern Michigan had prepared him to handle the pressures and expectations of the professional game.

Reflecting on his journey, Maxx understood that each challenge had served a purpose. They had shaped his character, built resilience, and instilled a belief in his abilities. The lessons learned from setbacks were as valuable as his victories. By embracing challenges, he not only grew as an athlete but also as a person. His college football career laid the groundwork for a promising career, demonstrating that success is often born from overcoming adversity and remaining steadfast in pursuing one's dreams. The culmination of his hard work and breakthroughs on the field would soon set the stage for the next chapter of his life in professional football.

Preparing for the NFL Draft

As Maxx Crosby's collegiate career ended, the looming NFL Draft became the focus of his aspirations. This pivotal moment represented a culmination of years of hard work and the beginning of a new chapter filled with possibilities and uncertainties. Preparing for the NFL Draft is a multifaceted process beyond just physical training; it involves a combination of mental readiness, strategic planning, and navigating the intricacies of the selection process.

Maxx began his preparation with a rigorous training regimen to enhance his skills and showcase his abilities. He worked closely with trainers who specialized in preparing athletes for the demands of professional football. This phase included intense workouts focused on strength, speed, and agility to optimize his physical performance. Each day was filled with drills that tested his endurance, explosiveness, and overall athleticism. As he pushed his body to the limits, he learned the importance of consistency and discipline. Every repetition in the gym was a step closer to achieving his dream.

Beyond physical training, Maxx recognized the significance of honing his technical skills. He reviewed game film meticulously, analyzing his performances and those of top players in the league. This analysis allowed him to understand the nuances of various positions, particularly that of an edge rusher. He studied the techniques employed by successful professionals, learning how they leveraged their strengths and managed their weaknesses. Through this process, Maxx developed a clearer picture of what was required at the next level, and he adapted his training to emulate the best practices he observed.

The mental aspect of preparation played an equally important role. The pressure and scrutiny surrounding the NFL Draft can be overwhelming, and Maxx sought to cultivate a resilient mindset. He engaged in visualization exercises, imagining himself excelling in various scenarios during workouts and the draft day. These mental rehearsals helped him build confidence and reduce anxiety, allowing him to approach the process with a positive attitude. He understood that self-belief would be crucial when facing the draft's competitive environment and the challenges ahead.

As the draft approached, Maxx was invited to participate in the NFL Combine, a week-long showcase where college prospects demonstrate their skills in front of NFL coaches, scouts, and executives. This event is a crucial opportunity for players to make a lasting impression, and Maxx knew it was his chance to shine. He dedicated countless hours to preparing for the various drills he would face, including the 40-yard dash, bench press, vertical jump, and agility tests. Each drill required precision and strategy, and Maxx worked tirelessly to perfect his technique.

Arriving at the Combine, Maxx felt a mix of excitement and nervousness. The atmosphere was electric, filled with talented athletes vying for the same goal. As he moved through each event, he channeled his preparation into performance. The 40-yard dash was pivotal, as speed is a critical attribute for an edge rusher. Maxx focused on explosive starts and efficient running mechanics, knowing that every fraction of a second mattered. The adrenaline coursing through him propelled him forward, and as he crossed the finish line, he felt a rush of accomplishment.

In addition to the physical assessments, the Combine included interviews with NFL teams. These conversations were essential for coaches and executives to gauge a player's character, work ethic, and organizational fit. Maxx took these interviews seriously, approaching each session with authenticity and a willingness to share his journey. He spoke candidly about his experiences in college, challenges, and commitment to improving both on and off the field. His passion for the game and his desire to contribute to a team shone through, leaving a lasting impression on those who interviewed him.

Following the Combine, the focus shifted to individual team workouts and pro days. Maxx participated in workouts designed to showcase his skills for scouts and coaches. He knew that these sessions were critical for solidifying his draft position. In preparation for these events, he tailored his workouts to highlight his strengths, ensuring that he demonstrated his abilities in the best possible light. With each workout, he felt a growing sense of determination, fueled by the dream of playing in the NFL.

As the draft day drew nearer, Maxx faced moments of reflection. He thought about his sacrifices and the unwavering support from his family and friends throughout his journey. The late nights spent training, the early mornings in the gym, and the moments of doubt were all part of a larger narrative that had shaped him into the player he had become. This introspection fueled his motivation and reminded him to stay grounded amid the excitement.

The actual draft day was a whirlwind of emotions. As teams made their selections, Maxx anxiously waited for his name to be called. The anticipation was palpable, and he gathered with family and close friends, all of whom shared in the excitement of the moment. Each pick felt like an eternity, with the tension building as time passed. Finally, a wave of joy washed over him when his name echoed through the room. This was the moment he had worked for, the culmination of years of dedication and effort.

Joining an NFL team was a dream come true, but Maxx understood that the journey was far from over. He recognized that the transition to professional football would bring its own set of challenges. With excitement and determination, he prepared to embrace the new responsibilities and expectations that awaited him. His hard work preparing for the draft gave him the skills and mindset needed to navigate the path ahead.

As he stepped into this new chapter, Maxx remained committed to continuous improvement. He knew that the competition in the NFL was fierce, and complacency was not an option. The lessons learned during his college years, coupled with the preparation for the draft, would serve as a foundation for his future success. Each practice, each game, and each challenge would be opportunities to grow and further establish himself in the league.

Maxx Crosby's preparation for the NFL Draft exemplified the dedication and resilience required to succeed at the highest level of football. His journey from a young athlete in Colleyville, Texas, to a draft prospect ready to make his mark in the NFL is a testament to the power of hard work and perseverance. With the draft behind him and a professional career on the horizon, he was ready to embrace the challenges and opportunities ahead, fully aware that pursuing excellence was a lifelong endeavor.

Chapter 3: The NFL Draft and Joining the Raiders

A Fourth-Round Pick with First-Round Talent

Maxx Crosby entered the NFL Draft with a mixture of hope and determination, armed with the skills and drive that had propelled him through college football. Despite the impressive stats and highlights showcasing his potential, he was selected in the fourth round, a decision that left many analysts and fans scratching their heads. The prevailing sentiment among observers was that Maxx possessed first-round talent, yet various factors led to his drop in the draft. This paradoxical situation became a significant aspect of his early career narrative.

As the draft unfolded, teams made selections based on various criteria, including immediate needs, potential upside, and fit within their systems. While Maxx had shown considerable promise on the field, questions lingered regarding his consistency and how he would translate his college success professionally. Some scouts raised concerns about his technique and whether he could consistently dominate against elite competition. These factors and the team's strategies and preferences ultimately contributed to his fourth-round status.

Upon being drafted by the Las Vegas Raiders, Maxx faced the dual challenge of proving himself and overcoming the perception that he had been overlooked. Joining an NFL franchise comes with inherent pressures, especially for a player viewed as a late-round selection. Many would consider this an uphill battle, but Maxx approached the situation unwaveringly. He understood that being underestimated could serve as motivation rather than a hindrance. The fire to prove doubters wrong burned brightly within him, propelling him to work harder.

The Raiders coaching staff recognized Maxx's potential and were eager to mold him into a key contributor. From day one of training camp, he threw himself into his work, determined to make an impact. The grueling practices tested his limits, yet Maxx embraced the challenge. He understood that the NFL was a different beast compared to college, with speed and intensity magnified exponentially. Each drill allowed him to refine his skills and demonstrate his worth.

While physical ability is crucial, football IQ plays a vital role in a player's success. Maxx made a concerted effort to soak up knowledge from his coaches and veteran teammates. He was particularly attentive during meetings, asking questions to deepen his understanding of defensive schemes and opposing offenses. This intellectual curiosity set him apart from many of his peers. He wanted to grasp his role and the entire defense's dynamics. By doing so, he could anticipate plays and react swiftly on the field, a skill that would serve him well as he adapted to the pro game.

As the preseason progressed, Maxx's hard work began to pay off. His natural athleticism and unrelenting work ethic caught the attention of coaches and fans alike. During practice sessions, he showcased an explosive first step off the line, exceptional agility, and a keen sense of timing. It became evident that he had the potential to disrupt opposing offenses consistently. Each practice felt like a stepping stone toward solidifying his place on the roster.

When the preseason games began, Maxx seized the opportunity to make his mark. His first appearance as a Raider was not just about wearing the jersey but proving that he belonged on that stage. As he stepped onto the field, the excitement and nerves coursed through him, but he channeled those feelings into performance. He delivered impressive tackles during the games, showing his ability to read plays and react quickly. His energy was infectious, and it resonated not just with fans but also with teammates who recognized his potential.

Amid these early successes, Maxx remained grounded, understanding that transitioning from college to the NFL required ongoing adaptation. He encountered challenges that tested his resolve, particularly against established offensive linemen. The speed and power of the game were unforgiving, and he occasionally found himself outmatched. However, Maxx analyzed these moments as learning experiences rather than succumbing to frustration. He worked tirelessly to improve his technique and develop strategies to counter the competition.

Maxx's ability to turn challenges into opportunities was crucial as he navigated the rigors of the NFL. The Raiders coaching staff provided constructive feedback, emphasizing improvement areas while acknowledging his strengths. Maxx took this input to heart, striving to become a more well-rounded player. He spent additional hours studying film, focusing on his footwork and hand placement to gain an advantage over blockers. His commitment to continuous improvement became a hallmark of his approach, setting a standard for himself and his teammates.

As the regular season approached, anticipation mounted. The moment Maxx had worked so hard for was finally within reach. When he received the news that he would be on the active roster, exhilaration filled him. It was a testament to his dedication and perseverance, affirming that hard work can yield results. However, with this achievement came a new set of challenges. The reality of playing in the NFL meant facing some of the best athletes in the world week after week.

Maxx's growth became evident during his rookie season as he took the field each game. He showcased flashes of brilliance that validated the belief many held in him, and there were moments when he shined brightly against top-tier opponents. The coaching staff began integrating him into crucial defensive packages, recognizing his ability to influence games. He developed a reputation as a player who could change the tide with key plays, whether through a pivotal sack or a crucial tackle.

Maxx quickly learned that consistency would be the key to establishing himself in the league. Each game was an opportunity to build on previous performances, and he approached each matchup with a sense of purpose. The lessons from earlier setbacks remained fresh in his mind, guiding him to stay focused and resilient. He embraced the grind of a full season, understanding that it was a marathon, not a sprint.

As the season progressed, discussions about Maxx's potential grew louder. Analysts highlighted his contributions, with many remarking that he played like a first-round pick. His performances and growing impact on the field garnered recognition, and the narrative surrounding him began to shift. The fourth-round selection that once raised eyebrows became a story of triumph and potential. Fans rallied around him, appreciating his tenacity and commitment to proving doubters wrong.

With the season approaching its conclusion, Maxx's journey became a source of inspiration for many aspiring athletes. His story exemplified that talent can be overlooked, but determination and work ethic can drive success. Maxx knew the importance of staying humble and acknowledging the support he had received from family, coaches, and teammates. Their belief in him fueled his desire to reach greater heights.

As the playoffs loomed, Maxx's focus sharpened. He recognized that this was an opportunity to leave an indelible mark in his rookie season. The possibility of competing on the grand stage ignited a fire within him. He committed himself to elevating his performance and preparing mentally and physically for the challenge. With each practice, he honed his skills, ensuring he would be ready for the intensity of playoff football.

Maxx Crosby's ascent from a fourth-round pick to a player who consistently demonstrated first-round talent is a testament to his resolve and dedication. His journey reminds him that talent may be recognized differently, but the work behind the scenes ultimately determines success. The challenges he faced only served to fuel his desire to excel. As he stood on the brink of playoff football, he carried with him the knowledge that the road ahead would require every ounce of effort and tenacity he had within him. Each game was not just a chance to compete; it was an opportunity to solidify his place in the NFL and showcase the talent that had always been there, waiting for the right moment to shine.

Making an Immediate Impact in His Rookie Season

Maxx Crosby's rookie season with the Las Vegas Raiders became a pivotal chapter in his burgeoning career, filled with unexpected challenges and moments of brilliance. From the outset, he was determined to prove himself and show that he was not just a fourth-round pick but a player capable of making significant contributions to his team. The anticipation surrounding his debut was palpable, and the Raiders coaching staff and fans alike were eager to see how he would perform on the professional stage.

As the regular season commenced, Maxx quickly established himself as a player who thrived under pressure. He displayed an impressive combination of speed, strength, and agility, making him formidable on the defensive line. Coaches recognized his potential, and he was given opportunities to showcase his skills in various defensive schemes. Maxx's ability to read plays and his explosive first step allowed him to disrupt opposing offenses right from his first game.

His first official appearance in the NFL came with excitement and nerves. Stepping onto the field, the atmosphere was electric. The crowd's roar, the bright lights, and the weight of expectations fueled him. As the game unfolded, he quickly adjusted to the pace and physicality of the league. Early in the game, he made his mark by tackling a running back in the backfield, sending a message that he was not there just to take part but to compete fiercely.

Maxx's relentless work ethic soon became evident as he consistently made plays that turned the tide in favor of the Raiders. In the following weeks, he emerged as a key player on the defensive line. His ability to pressure quarterbacks became one of his defining traits. Coaches emphasized the importance of getting to the quarterback quickly, and Maxx took that directive to heart. He studied the tendencies of opposing quarterbacks, learning how to anticipate their movements and react accordingly.

As the season progressed, his performance garnered attention from fans and analysts. He racked up tackles, sacks, and forced fumbles, with each play adding to his growing reputation. Maxx became known for his knack for creating turnovers, a crucial element that coaches sought in a player. His hunger to excel translated into results on the field, and the more he played, the more confidence he gained. Each tackle and sack fueled his desire to keep pushing the boundaries of his capabilities.

The camaraderie within the Raiders' locker room significantly impacted his transition to the NFL. Teammates recognized Maxx's talent and supported him through the ups and downs of the season. Veteran players took him under their wings, providing guidance and advice on navigating the challenges of being a professional athlete. These relationships were invaluable, as they fostered growth and learning.

Despite the challenges of a rookie season, Maxx demonstrated a remarkable ability to adapt. He learned from his mistakes and was not afraid to ask questions when uncertain. His coaches praised his willingness to absorb feedback, which enabled him to refine his technique and approach to the game. Maxx's growth was not solely based on his physical attributes but also on his football intelligence.

He quickly grasped the nuances of defensive play, allowing him to anticipate opposing offenses' strategies.

As the games continued, Maxx's impact became increasingly evident. He contributed to the field band and became a leader among his peers. His passion for the game and tireless work ethic inspired those around him. He understood the importance of leading by example, and his commitment to improving individually and as a team player resonated with his teammates. Maxx's infectious energy on and off the field fostered a competitive spirit that permeated the locker room.

One of the highlights of his rookie season was a standout performance against a highly-ranked offense. Maxx's determination was palpable as he prepared for the challenge, studying game tape and focusing on the opposing team's strengths and weaknesses. When the game day arrived, he played with an intensity that captivated everyone watching. He recorded multiple sacks and played a pivotal role in stifling the opposing team's run game. It was a performance showcasing his talent and potential, reaffirming that he was a player to watch in the league.

Maxx's statistics reflected his growth and development as the season neared. He ranked among the top rookies in the league for tackles and sacks, and discussions about his performance filled sports media. Analysts began to highlight him as a player who could make a significant impact for years to come, and he earned a reputation as a rising star in the league. The accolades were gratifying, but Maxx remained grounded, focusing on the work ahead.

He understood that success in the NFL was not just about individual accolades but about contributing to the team's overall success. The Raiders aimed to make a deep playoff run, and Maxx was determined to play a pivotal role in that journey. His commitment to his teammates and the organization drove him to elevate his game further. Each practice became an opportunity to refine his skills and prepare for the challenges that awaited him in the playoffs.

As he approached the season's final stretch, Maxx reflected on his journey thus far. The challenges he faced, from being drafted later than expected to proving himself in a new environment, were formative experiences. These trials shaped his character and fueled his desire to succeed. He understood that every moment spent on the field was a chance to showcase the hard work and dedication that had defined his path.

Maxx Crosby's rookie season was a testament to his talent, work ethic, and resilience. He transformed from a fourth-round pick into a player who made an immediate impact, earning respect and admiration from teammates and fans alike. The skills he displayed and the leadership he exhibited laid the foundation for what promised to be a remarkable career. As the season ended, the anticipation for what lay ahead grew stronger. Maxx had proven himself on the field and established himself as a key figure in the Raiders' future, ready to face whatever challenges the next season would bring. His journey was just beginning, and he was determined to continue making strides as he aimed for greatness in the NFL.

Earning Respect as an NFL Newcomer

Entering the NFL as a newcomer is often filled with excitement and uncertainty. For Maxx Crosby, the journey to earning respect in the league was a mixture of proving his capabilities on the field and assimilating into the professional football culture. With every practice and game, he faced the challenge of establishing himself as a player to be reckoned with while navigating the complexities of a new environment.

From the beginning of his rookie season, Maxx understood the importance of making a strong impression. He knew that the NFL is a league where talent alone does not guarantee respect. It requires a combination of skill, work ethic, and the ability to earn the trust of teammates and coaches. He approached each practice with relentless determination, showcasing his ability to absorb feedback and apply it immediately. This eagerness to learn quickly caught the attention of his coaches, who recognized his potential to develop into a key player.

His first days in the locker room were both exhilarating and intimidating. Surrounded by established stars and veterans, Maxx knew he had to navigate the intricate dynamics of the team. He made it a point to introduce himself and engage with his teammates, eager to build rapport. Many veterans offered him advice, sharing insights about what it takes to thrive in the league. This guidance became invaluable as he adjusted to the speed and intensity of the game. Still, it was also essential for forming the relationships that would underpin his respect within the team.

Maxx's determination on the field was evident from his very first practice. He approached drills with a focus that demonstrated his commitment to improving. Coaches took notice of his relentless pursuit of perfection, often praising his energy and effort. Maxx consistently pushed himself, whether sprinting during conditioning drills or giving maximum effort in one-on-one matchups. This tenacity resonated with his teammates, who appreciated his willingness to leave everything on the field.

As the regular season unfolded, Maxx faced the typical challenges that accompany a rookie's transition into professional football. He experienced ups and downs, from exciting plays that drew cheers from the crowd to moments of frustration when things did not go as planned. Despite these challenges, he maintained a positive attitude, using each experience as a learning opportunity. This resilience earned him admiration from those around him, as teammates recognized that he was someone who would not be easily discouraged.

In addition to his work ethic, Maxx's ability to perform under pressure sets him apart. He thrived in crucial moments, stepping up when his team needed him most. Whether chasing down a quarterback in a pivotal game or making a crucial tackle on third down, he demonstrated that he could be counted on when the stakes were high. Such performances solidified his role on the defense and showed his teammates that he would rise to the occasion.

Building trust among teammates extended beyond mere performance; it was also about demonstrating a strong character. Maxx made it a point to support his fellow players, celebrating their successes and encouraging them during difficult times. This camaraderie was essential in establishing a sense of unity within the team. He laid the groundwork for a collaborative and cohesive defense by fostering an environment of mutual respect.

As the season progressed, Maxx's hard work began to pay off. He started to gain recognition within the Raiders organization and across the league. Analysts began to take note of his impact on the field, highlighting his statistics and contributions in various games. Being labeled a promising rookie brought a new level of attention and expectations. Rather than allowing the accolades to inflate his ego, Maxx remained grounded, focusing on the aspects of his game that still required improvement.

The feedback from coaches and teammates reinforced his determination. They emphasized that respect is earned through talent, consistency, and professionalism. Maxx took this to heart, approaching every practice and game with the same enthusiasm. He was committed to refining his technique and learning from the veterans around him. This attitude resonated throughout the locker room, and soon, he was regarded not only as a rising star but also as a valuable member of the team's culture.

One of the defining moments of his rookie season came when he delivered a standout performance against a formidable opponent. The pressure was palpable, but Maxx approached the game with a steely focus. He remembered the preparation leading up to it, from studying game film to collaborating with his coaches on strategies. When the game began, he unleashed his skills, recording multiple tackles and making a critical sack that shifted the momentum in favor of the Raiders. After the game, the praise from his coaches and teammates affirmed his standing as a player who had earned their respect.

As the weeks turned into months, Maxx's reputation continued to grow. He embraced the role of a competitor and a leader. His peers often looked to him for motivation during practices, and his presence alone became a source of inspiration. He encouraged his teammates to push themselves, fostering a competitive atmosphere that elevated the unit. This leadership quality, combined with his natural talent, established him as someone who commanded respect on and off the field.

With the season approaching its climax, Maxx reflected on his journey. The challenges he faced, both personally and professionally, had shaped his character. He had learned valuable lessons about the importance of humility, perseverance, and the power of teamwork. As he prepared for the next game, he remained committed to his growth, focusing on the elements of his game that still required attention.

Maxx Crosby's ability to earn respect as an NFL newcomer was a testament to his dedication, talent, and the relationships he built along the way. He transformed from a young player entering the league with questions about his potential into a respected figure within the Raiders organization. His rookie season laid the foundation for what promised to be a successful career characterized by hard work, resilience, and an unwavering commitment to excellence. As he looked ahead, the knowledge that he had earned the respect of his teammates and coaches only fueled his ambition to continue striving for greatness in the NFL.

Chapter 4: Breakout Season and Early Success

Surpassing Expectations with 10 Sacks in Rookie Year

As Maxx Crosby embarked on his rookie season, expectations were high but varied among fans, analysts, and coaches alike. Drafted in the fourth round, many viewed him as a potential hidden gem for the Las Vegas Raiders, but questions lingered about how quickly he could adapt to the rigors of the NFL. Despite being a late-round pick, Maxx approached the season with an unyielding determination to prove himself, focusing on the hard work necessary to surpass any preconceived limitations placed upon him.

The start of the season was a whirlwind of excitement and nerves, with each game serving as an opportunity for Maxx to showcase his skills. He quickly became familiar with the intensity and speed of professional football, immersing himself in the playbook and absorbing insights from veteran teammates. From the very first snap of the season, he displayed a fierce competitive spirit that caught the attention of coaches and teammates alike. As he worked through training camp and preseason games, it became evident that he possessed the talent and drive to make a significant impact.

Crosby's relentless pursuit of quarterbacks was evident from his very first game. In those early weeks, he found himself adjusting to the nuances of the position, learning how to read offensive formations and anticipate plays. His early performances were a mix of raw energy and eagerness to prove himself, often leading to impressive plays and occasional mistakes. However, each setback became a lesson, teaching him how to refine his technique and make smarter decisions on the field.

Maxx's breakout moment came during the season's second game. With his confidence building, he put together a performance that solidified his position on the roster and hinted at the potential for greatness. He recorded his first sack, and the electrifying feeling surged through him. The crowd's roar as he brought down the opposing quarterback resonated deeply, reinforcing his belief that he could achieve even more. Following that game, he felt the weight of expectations lift slightly as the coaching staff began to take note of his potential.

As the weeks progressed, Crosby's performance began to improve markedly. He honed his skills, focusing on techniques to maximize his effectiveness as a pass rusher. The film sessions became a critical part of his routine, as he meticulously studied opposing offenses, analyzing the tendencies of quarterbacks and offensive linemen. He recognized the value of preparation, understanding that it was the cornerstone of success in the league. This dedication did not go unnoticed; coaches praised his commitment and encouraged him to continue pushing boundaries.

The turning point in Crosby's rookie campaign arrived when he began to develop a signature playing style. He became adept at getting past offensive linemen using a combination of speed, agility, and strength. His long arms and quick first step allowed him to break through blocks and pressure quarterbacks, leading to impressive performances. Each sack he achieved was a personal victory and a testament to his hard work and determination to exceed expectations.

The support from teammates also played a pivotal role in Maxx's development. As a rookie, he was surrounded by seasoned veterans who recognized his potential and younger players who looked up to him. The camaraderie within the team fostered an environment conducive to growth. Maxx was learning from their experiences and drawing inspiration from their work ethic. This collective energy helped him thrive, pushing him to be his best version.

By midseason, the narrative surrounding Maxx began to shift. He was no longer seen merely as a promising rookie but became a crucial element of the Raiders' defense. His name began in discussions about standout performers with each passing game. Analysts began to take note of his statistics, highlighting his rapidly accumulating sacks. What started as whispers of potential transformed into a chorus of recognition as he solidified his status as one of the league's top rookie defenders.

One of the most memorable moments of his rookie year came during a pivotal game against a divisional rival. The atmosphere was electric, with playoff implications on the line. As the game progressed, Maxx felt an intense surge of adrenaline, knowing that his performance could significantly impact the outcome. Throughout the contest, he consistently pressured the quarterback, leading to two crucial sacks that helped secure a hard-fought victory for the Raiders. The thrill of contributing to a team win solidified his passion for the game and fueled his desire to achieve even more.

As the season approached its conclusion, Maxx had achieved a remarkable milestone: ten sacks in his rookie year. This accomplishment exceeded all expectations, particularly for a player drafted in the fourth round. Each sack represented a statistic and a moment of triumph, showcasing his growth and determination. The achievement validated the hard work he had put in, earning him respect not only from his teammates but also from coaches and fans alike.

Reflecting on the season, Maxx recognized the significance of his success. The journey from being an overlooked draft pick to becoming a key player in the league was a testament to his unwavering commitment. He understood that achieving ten sacks was not merely a number; it was a reflection of the countless hours spent honing his skills, learning from his mistakes, and pushing through the challenges that came his way. The resilience he displayed throughout the season reinforced the notion that he belonged among the elite players in the league.

Looking ahead, Maxx was excited about the future. The ten sacks were just the beginning, and he envisioned a career filled with continued growth and achievements. He knew that with each passing season, he had the opportunity to evolve as a player, refining his techniques and expanding his skill set. The support of his teammates, coupled with his relentless drive, positioned him to become a talented player and a leader on and off the field.

In the following months, as he prepared for the challenges of the next season, Maxx carried with him the lessons learned during his rookie year. His dedication to continuous improvement, the importance of teamwork, and the power of perseverance became the guiding principles for his future endeavors. He was determined to build upon his success, eager to prove that his rookie season was not merely a flash in the pan but the foundation for a lasting legacy in the NFL.

Maxx Crosby's journey from an unheralded fourth-round pick to a standout rookie with ten sacks was a story of determination, resilience, and hard work. Each game, each practice, and each moment contributed to a narrative that was just beginning. As he looked forward to the future, he knew that the sky was the limit, and he was ready to take on the challenges ahead, fully aware that surpassing expectations was merely the first step on a much larger path to greatness.

Recognition in the NFL All-Rookie Team

As the NFL season progressed, Maxx Crosby's impressive performance caught the attention of fans, analysts, and fellow players. His remarkable ten sacks during his rookie year, coupled with a relentless style of play, showcased a level of talent many believed would elevate him to greater heights in the league. The recognition came when the NFL All-Rookie Team was announced, a prestigious accolade highlighting the top first-year players in the league. This recognition was a significant milestone for Maxx, validating his hard work and determination throughout the season.

The All-Rookie Team is comprised of players who excelled statistically and demonstrated consistent performance on the field. As the list was unveiled, excitement surged among the Raiders' fanbase and within the team. When Maxx's name was announced, it was a moment of joy for him and everyone who had supported him along the way. His achievement resonated deeply, symbolizing the culmination of his efforts and the faith that the coaching staff had placed in him from the beginning.

Being named to the All-Rookie Team was particularly meaningful for Maxx, as it underscored that he had earned his place among the best newcomers in the league. Players chosen for this honor often went on to have significant careers. For Maxx, it was an opportunity to showcase that he was not just a one-hit wonder but rather a player who could continue contributing to his team's success for years. The accolade served as both a recognition of his accomplishments and a motivation to keep pushing forward.

The media coverage surrounding his selection was intense. Sports networks and websites featured analysis of his rookie season, praising his technique, work ethic, and ability to make impactful plays. Analysts highlighted his knack for getting to the quarterback and how he disrupted opposing offenses. Each highlight reel showcased his ability to pressure quarterbacks, a hallmark of his play style. As the praises rolled in, Maxx remained grounded, focused on his roots and the people who had helped him reach this point.

The celebration of his achievement also brought attention to the Raiders organization. Despite being a fourth-round pick, the team's investment in drafting Crosby had proven fruitful. This recognition amplified the narrative surrounding the franchise's ability to identify and develop talent. It became a source of pride for the Raiders, who had faced challenges in previous seasons. Maxx's success revitalized discussions about the potential for the team to build a competitive roster capable of contending for championships in the future.

Maxx took the time to reflect on the journey that had led him to this recognition. He remembered the long hours of practice, the grueling training sessions, and the sacrifices he had made along the way. The dedication shown by his family, coaches, and teammates played a vital role in shaping him into the player he had become. Being honored as part of the All-Rookie Team allowed him to express gratitude to those who supported him. He understood that this accolade was not solely his achievement but a testament to the collective efforts of everyone who had influenced his life and career. The recognition also gave Maxx newfound confidence as he prepared for the following season. It confirmed that the hard work put into his craft was paying off and encouraged him to strive for heights. His aspirations shifted toward becoming a more complete player. With his rookie season behind him, Maxx aimed to refine his techniques, increase his sack numbers, and make an even more significant impact on the field. The weight of expectation now rested on his shoulders, but he welcomed the challenge with open arms, knowing that he had the support of his teammates and coaches.

As the offseason approached, Maxx took this opportunity to set personal goals. He sought to enhance his physical conditioning and focus on areas that could elevate his game. Training sessions during the offseason became critical in ensuring he was ready for the upcoming season. He worked diligently to improve his speed, strength, and agility, determined to build upon the foundation laid during his rookie year. Maxx recognized that while being named to the All-Rookie Team was an incredible honor, sustaining that level of performance required relentless dedication and commitment.

The bond formed with his teammates during the season also contributed to his growth as a player. They pushed one another in practice, holding each other accountable and providing valuable feedback. Learning from veteran players became an integral part of his development. Their insights about the game's nuances allowed Maxx to elevate his understanding of football strategy and situational awareness. This mentorship solidified a strong team dynamic, fostering an environment where younger players felt empowered to take risks and pursue excellence.

Maxx also embraced the opportunity to give back to the community that supported him throughout his journey. He recognized the significance of his platform as a professional athlete and sought ways to inspire young athletes in his hometown and beyond. Engaging with local schools and youth programs became a priority. Sharing his experiences helped him connect with aspiring football players who looked up to him. He understood the importance of representation and aimed to instill a sense of hope and determination in the next generation.

As the new season approached, Maxx felt the weight of anticipation building. The recognition of being named to the All-Rookie Team fueled his competitive spirit. He knew the next challenge was establishing himself as a cornerstone of the Raiders' defense. The accolades and attention would only increase with success, and he was ready to embrace the responsibilities of being a key player in the NFL.

The announcement of his inclusion in the All-Rookie Team transformed the narrative surrounding Maxx Crosby. From an overlooked draft choice to a celebrated performer, he had defied the odds. As he prepared to step onto the field again, he carried the lessons learned from his rookie season, the support of those who believed in him, and an unwavering determination to prove that he was just getting started. This recognition was a reflection of past success and a stepping stone toward a promising future filled with endless possibilities. Each game was an opportunity to solidify his place in the league and carve out a legacy far beyond his rookie season.

Establishing Himself as a Key Defensive Asset

As Maxx Crosby entered his second season in the NFL, the expectations surrounding him grew significantly. After making a strong impact during his rookie year and earning recognition as a standout performer, he understood that maintaining and building upon that success would be critical. The second season often serves as a pivotal point for many players, and Maxx was determined to prove that his impressive debut was not just a flash in the pan.

One of his first steps was to assess his performance from the previous year. Reflecting on his play, Maxx identified areas where he could improve. While he had garnered attention for his ability to rush the passer, he recognized that becoming a well-rounded defensive player was essential. This meant focusing on sacks, stopping the run, and reading offensive formations more effectively. Maxx studied game film, analyzing his plays and those of opposing players and defenses. This strategic approach allowed him to understand different play styles and anticipate what offenses might try to do against him.

Maxx's commitment to improvement extended beyond film study. He dedicated himself to an intensive training regimen during the offseason. Working closely with strength and conditioning coaches, he aimed to enhance his physical attributes, focusing on strength, speed, and agility. The training sessions were grueling, but Maxx welcomed the challenge, understanding that the physical demands of the NFL were unlike any other. He sought to increase his explosiveness off the line of scrimmage, a crucial factor in getting to the quarterback before they could release the ball. Each day in the gym and on the practice field was a step toward solidifying his role as a vital asset on defense.

As the preseason approached, the excitement in the air was palpable. Teammates and coaches alike recognized Maxx's dedication and growth. During training camp, he displayed an impressive work ethic, pushing through fatigue and consistently bringing energy to practices. This attitude resonated with his teammates, fostering a spirit of competition and camaraderie. They observed his determination to lead the defensive line, and many sought to follow his example. This unity proved essential as the team prepared for the upcoming challenges of the regular season.

Once the season began, Maxx quickly established himself as a key defensive asset. Each game showcased his evolving skill set and determination. His ability to pressure quarterbacks became a focal point of the Raiders' defensive strategy. Coordinators devised schemes that leveraged his speed and tenacity, allowing him to exploit favored matchups. Game after game, he consistently found ways to disrupt opposing offenses, whether through sacking the quarterback, forcing fumbles, or applying relentless pressure that led to hurried throws. The impact of his play was evident as opponents began to game-plan around him, often double-teaming or using tight ends to chip him on his rushes.

Beyond his contributions, Maxx embraced a leadership role within the defensive unit. He understood that to truly establish himself as a key asset, he needed to elevate those around him. This involved sharing insights and techniques with younger players, helping them adjust to the speed and complexity of the NFL. Maxx's approachable demeanor made him a respected figure in the locker room. Teammates felt comfortable seeking his advice, whether it pertained to specific plays or navigating the pressures of professional football. He recognized that fostering a collaborative atmosphere strengthened the defense and made it more cohesive.

Maxx's performance continued to draw fans and analysts' attention as the season progressed. His impressive statistics were complemented by his ability to make pivotal plays at crucial moments. Whether it was a key third-down stop or a momentum-shifting sack, he consistently rose to the occasion. These moments showcased his talent and solidified his reputation as a player who thrived under pressure. With each game, he earned respect from teammates and opponents who recognized his skill and determination.

Media coverage surrounding Maxx increased significantly as the season unfolded. Highlights of his plays circulated widely on social media, and analysts praised his technique and work ethic. As he navigated this newfound attention, he remained grounded, focused on his goals rather than the external noise. The accolades he received served as motivation rather than a distraction. He understood that the true measure of success lay in continued improvement and contributing to the team's overall performance.

Maxx's resilience was tested throughout the season. The physicality of the NFL took its toll, and he faced challenges, including minor injuries and the mental fatigue that often accompanies a grueling season. However, his dedication to recovery and maintaining peak physical condition allowed him to push through. He developed a robust routine that emphasized training and recovery strategies, such as massage therapy and mobility exercises. This commitment to self-care ensured he could perform at a high level week after week.

The support system surrounding Maxx played a significant role in his ability to thrive. His family remained a source of encouragement, attending games and celebrating his successes. They provided a grounding presence amid the chaos of the NFL, reminding him of the importance of humility and hard work. Teammates also rallied around him, creating an environment where everyone was committed to collective success. The bonds formed on and off the field contributed to a shared sense of purpose, allowing each player to push one another toward excellence.

By the season's conclusion, Maxx Crosby had established himself as a key defensive asset and positioned himself among the league's top performers. His skill, work ethic, and leadership set a standard within the Raiders' organization. The acknowledgment of his contributions came in various forms, from media recognition to the admiration of fans who appreciated his dedication and grit.

As Maxx reflected on his journey, he recognized the importance of continued growth. His challenges throughout the season were valuable learning experiences, reinforcing his desire to evolve as a player. He embraced the lessons from successes and setbacks, knowing that the path to greatness requires constant effort and adaptability.

With aspirations of reaching new heights in the NFL, Maxx remained committed to honing his craft. Each offseason presented an opportunity to further refine his skills, enhance his physical attributes, and build upon the foundation established in his early years as a professional athlete. The journey ahead would undoubtedly come with obstacles. Still, Maxx faced the future with determination and a strong sense of purpose, eager to leave his mark on the league and contribute to the Raiders' pursuit of success.

Chapter 5: Personal Struggles and Redemption

Facing Alcoholism and Entering Rehab

His athletic accomplishments did not solely define Maxx Crosby's journey in the NFL. It was marked by personal challenges that tested his resolve and commitment to his craft. While he quickly gained recognition for his talent on the field, the pressures of professional sports and the demands of public life began to take a toll on him. As he grappled with these stressors, he found himself facing an unexpected adversary: alcoholism.

The onset of his struggles with alcohol was gradual, almost imperceptible at first. What began as occasional social drinking after games with teammates transformed into a coping mechanism for the pressures he faced. The spotlight of the NFL can be intense, and for many players, the expectation to perform at an elite level can lead to immense stress and anxiety. Maxx was no different. While he worked tirelessly to enhance his performance and prove himself, the weight of those expectations affected him emotionally.

Initially, Maxx dismissed his drinking as a normal part of life as a professional athlete. Celebrations after victories or nights out with friends seemed harmless, even typical for someone in his position. However, as time passed, he noticed a pattern emerging. What should have been celebratory moments occasionally spiraled into excessive drinking. Social gatherings turned into opportunities for him to escape, and the very camaraderie that once brought him joy began to be overshadowed by his dependence on alcohol.

Recognizing the seriousness of his situation became a painful yet necessary realization. Maxx struggled with feelings of shame and denial, wrestling with the idea that he might be facing an addiction. It wasn't easy to confront the fact that something he had once viewed as a means of relaxation and celebration had become a crutch, affecting his personal life and professional commitments. He found himself in a vicious cycle, where alcohol provided a temporary escape but ultimately compounded his stress and anxiety.

The tipping point came during a particularly challenging stretch in the season. After a few tough losses, he felt overwhelmed by disappointment and frustration. Maxx turned to alcohol more frequently, believing it would help him forget the pressures of his performance. This only led to deeper issues, as he started to miss workouts and practices due to hangovers, causing friction with coaches and teammates. The relationships that once supported him became strained as his behavior changed. Teammates began to express their concerns, but Maxx brushed off their worries, believing he could manage the situation independently.

However, the facade he maintained began to crumble. The cumulative effects of his drinking habits began to manifest not only in his physical performance but also in his mental health. Moments of clarity became scarce, and he often felt trapped in a haze of self-doubt and anxiety. It was during this tumultuous period that he finally reached a breaking point. After a particularly difficult game, where he felt he let his team down, Maxx decided to confront his struggles head-on.

He reached out to close friends and family members, sharing his battle with alcohol and the toll it had taken on his life. Their support proved invaluable, as they encouraged him to seek professional help. Opening up was cathartic, yet it also marked the beginning of a challenging road to recovery. Maxx understood that acknowledging the problem was merely the first step; the journey ahead would require dedication and a willingness to confront his demons.

Entering rehab was a pivotal moment for Maxx. He found himself in an environment designed for healing, surrounded by individuals who understood the complexities of addiction. The initial days were filled with uncertainty, but as he engaged with therapists and fellow patients, he began to grasp the underlying issues that contributed to his dependence. The structured routines, along with group therapy sessions, allowed him to express his feelings in a safe space and gain insights into the psychological aspects of addiction.

Maxx learned about the triggers that fueled his drinking, exploring the connection between his emotional state and his alcohol use. He came to realize that he had often turned to alcohol as a way to cope with stress rather than addressing the root causes. This realization opened his eyes to the importance of developing healthier coping mechanisms. He engaged in discussions about mindfulness, resilience, and the significance of emotional regulation. These tools not only helped him confront his addiction but also provided strategies for navigating the pressures of his career.

During his time in rehab, Maxx also began reconnecting with his passions outside of football. He had often defined himself solely by his athletic achievements, but in recovery, he discovered the importance of nurturing other aspects of his identity. Art, writing, and physical fitness became outlets for expression, allowing him to channel his emotions in productive ways. This newfound balance helped him understand that he was more than just a football player; he was a multifaceted individual capable of pursuing various interests and passions.

As he progressed through the program, Maxx found strength in vulnerability. He shared his experiences with others, encouraging them to confront their struggles. His willingness to be open about his challenges fostered a sense of community among the participants. They created a support network where they could lean on each other during difficult moments and celebrate each other's victories, no matter how small. This camaraderie became a crucial element of his healing process.

Completing the rehab program marked a significant milestone in Maxx's journey. Armed with a renewed sense of purpose, he was determined to return to the NFL as a player and advocate for mental health and addiction recovery. He realized his experience could be a powerful example for others facing similar challenges. This commitment to advocacy became a driving force in his life, motivating him to share his story openly and inspire others to seek help.

Upon returning to the Raiders, Maxx faced the dual challenge of reintegrating into the team and continuing his recovery. The transition was not without obstacles; old habits and environments could trigger feelings of temptation and nostalgia. However, he approached these challenges with newfound resilience. Maxx established a support system among his teammates, confiding in those who had shown concern during his struggles. Their encouragement reminded him that he was not alone in his journey.

Maxx embraced his role as a player and mentor as the season progressed. He began speaking publicly about his experiences with alcoholism, raising awareness about the importance of mental health in professional sports. His willingness to share his story resonated with fans and fellow athletes alike, emphasizing that vulnerability could be a source of strength. Maxx's openness helped break down the stigma surrounding addiction, encouraging others to seek help rather than suffer in silence.

Facing alcoholism and entering rehab was a defining chapter in Maxx Crosby's life. It transformed his understanding of himself and his place in the world of sports. No longer just a talented athlete, he emerged as a voice for change, advocating for mental health awareness and the importance of support systems. The experience underscored that even the most talented individuals can face profound struggles. By embracing his journey, Maxx found a path to recovery and became a beacon of hope for others navigating similar battles. His story serves as a reminder that it's never too late to confront one's demons and seek a better future, proving that resilience and strength can emerge from the depths of personal challenges.

Commitment to Sobriety and Personal Growth

Maxx Crosby's journey toward sobriety was marked by a profound transformation, intertwining his commitment to personal growth with his career in the NFL. After completing rehab, he faced the challenge of re-entering the high-pressure world of professional football, armed with a newfound sense of purpose and determination. Sobriety was not merely a goal but a fundamental shift in how he approached his life, relationships, and responsibilities.

Initially, the path of sobriety was filled with uncertainty and apprehension. Maxx understood that he was entering an environment fraught with potential triggers and pressures. The atmosphere of professional sports often glorifies a party lifestyle, and he knew that navigating this world would require vigilance and resolve. However, rather than viewing these challenges as obstacles, Maxx began to see them as opportunities for personal growth. He made a conscious decision to adopt a proactive approach to his sobriety, ensuring that he surrounded himself with positivity and support.

Maxx recognized the importance of building a solid foundation for his new life. He began attending support groups regularly, connecting with others who shared similar experiences. This network provided not only accountability but also a sense of belonging. He realized that being part of a community that understood the intricacies of addiction and recovery was invaluable. Listening to the stories of others, he found inspiration and comfort, reminding him that he was not alone in his struggles.

In addition to attending meetings, Maxx committed himself to therapy, where he explored the deeper issues that contributed to his reliance on alcohol. These sessions offered a safe space to unpack his feelings and experiences, helping him to understand the underlying triggers for his past behavior. Through this process, he developed healthier coping mechanisms to deal with stress, anxiety, and the pressures of being a professional athlete. This self-exploration allowed him to address the emotional wounds he had long avoided, facilitating healing that would underpin his journey toward sobriety.

Maxx also turned his attention to physical fitness with renewed vigor. While he had always been dedicated to training, his commitment now had a different meaning. Fitness became a crucial outlet for his energy and emotions, a natural antidote to his challenges. He established a rigorous training regimen that enhanced his athletic performance and fostered a sense of discipline and accomplishment. The physical exertion gave him clarity and focus, allowing him to channel his determination into every aspect of his life.

As he worked diligently on his sobriety, Maxx became increasingly aware of the impact of nutrition and overall wellness on his mental health. He educated himself about healthy eating habits and made conscious choices to fuel his body with nutritious foods. This commitment to wellness extended beyond physical fitness; it encompassed mindfulness practices such as meditation and yoga. These practices became integral to his daily routine, offering him tools to manage stress and promote emotional balance.

Maxx cultivated strong relationships with mentors and teammates who supported his growth throughout his journey. He recognized the importance of surrounding himself with individuals who encouraged his sobriety and understood his goals. Their unwavering support provided a sense of accountability and motivation, reminding him of his progress. Maxx often engaged in open conversations with his teammates about his experiences, fostering an environment of vulnerability and trust. By sharing his journey, he reinforced his commitment to sobriety and inspired others to be more mindful of their health and well-being.

As the season progressed, Maxx became a vocal advocate for mental health awareness within the NFL community. He leveraged his platform to address the stigma surrounding addiction and recovery, emphasizing that seeking help is a sign of strength, not weakness. Through community outreach programs and partnerships with organizations dedicated to mental health, he aimed to raise awareness and promote resources for those in need. His story resonated with fans and fellow athletes, proving that personal struggles can lead to transformative change.

Maxx's commitment to sobriety also influenced his performance on the field. He played at an elite level as he honed his skills and focused on his physical and mental health. His dedication to the game was evident, and he approached each practice and game with a newfound intensity. This transformation did not go unnoticed; coaches and teammates praised his work ethic and determination. He inspired those around him, embodying the idea that personal growth can enhance individual performance and the team's overall success.

In addition to his on-field performance, Maxx began to explore opportunities for personal development beyond football. He pursued educational opportunities aligned with his interests, particularly in mental health and wellness. This pursuit of knowledge fueled his desire to make a meaningful impact on the lives of others. By equipping himself with information and understanding, he aimed to contribute positively to the conversations surrounding mental health in sports and beyond.

As Maxx continued navigating life's complexities in the NFL, he remained committed to his sobriety and personal growth. He understood that recovery is a lifelong journey requiring continuous effort and dedication. Each day presented challenges and victories; he approached them with resilience and determination. He learned to celebrate small achievements, recognizing that every step forward was significant.

The influence of his experiences extended beyond his own life. Maxx actively participated in community service initiatives, using his platform to give back to those in need. He understood that his journey had equipped him with valuable insights and empathy, allowing him to connect with individuals facing their struggles. Whether speaking at schools, engaging with youth programs, or participating in charity events, he embraced opportunities to share his story and uplift others.

Maxx Crosby's commitment to sobriety and personal growth became a defining aspect of his identity. It shaped his approach to football and his outlook on life. He learned that vulnerability could coexist with strength and that his past struggles could become a source of empowerment. Embracing his journey, he transformed his life and inspired those around him to prioritize their well-being and pursue their growth paths.

As he reflected on his journey, Maxx understood that his experiences had forged a deeper sense of purpose. He recognized the importance of staying connected to his support network, remaining engaged in his recovery, and continuing to advocate for mental health awareness. Maxx's story serves as a testament to the power of resilience, illustrating that it is possible to overcome adversity and emerge stronger on the other side with commitment and determination. Each day became an opportunity for growth, a chance to reaffirm his commitment to sobriety, and a reminder that personal transformation is a journey worth pursuing.

Becoming a Mental Health Advocate

Maxx Crosby's evolution into a mental health advocate represents a pivotal chapter in his life, blending his personal experiences with a profound commitment to effecting positive change in the lives of others. Emerging from the shadows of his struggles with alcoholism, he recognized a unique opportunity to leverage his platform as an

NFL player to spark conversations about mental health and addiction. His journey from a troubled athlete to an influential advocate reflects a deep understanding of mental well-being's complexities, particularly within the high-stakes world of professional sports.

His advocacy journey began as he navigated his recovery. Maxx experienced firsthand the stigma and isolation often associated with mental health issues. During his recovery process, he encountered numerous individuals battling similar challenges, and this exposure opened his eyes to the critical need for a supportive community. Many athletes grappling with the pressures of their careers often feel reluctant to seek help. They fear judgment or may believe that vulnerability could compromise their professional image. Maxx understood that if he could share his journey openly, it might encourage others to take the courageous step of seeking support.

With this realization, he decided to speak openly about his struggles, aiming to dismantle the stigma surrounding mental health in sports. He began sharing his story through interviews, social media, and community events, emphasizing the importance of honesty and vulnerability. His candid discussions about his experiences with alcohol and the subsequent journey to sobriety resonated deeply with fans and fellow athletes alike. He articulated a message throughout the sports community: it is okay not to be okay. Acknowledging one's struggles is the first step toward healing and growth.

Maxx's approach to advocacy was rooted in authenticity. He did not shy away from discussing the difficulties he faced, nor did he present a polished, unrealistic image of recovery. Instead, he painted a picture of the hard work, setbacks, and victories that define the journey toward mental wellness. This raw honesty endeared him to many, creating a safe space for conversations about mental health. People began to reach out, sharing their stories and thanking him for being a voice in a landscape that often felt silenced.

Recognizing that advocacy was more than just sharing his story, Maxx took proactive steps to educate himself about mental health issues. He sought to understand the various dimensions of mental health, addiction, and recovery. This quest for knowledge led him to collaborate with mental health organizations and professionals. He participated in workshops, attended seminars, and engaged with mental health advocates to enhance his understanding of effective communication strategies and available resources to those in need.

Maxx also understood the importance of reaching out to young athletes, who face immense pressure to perform at high levels. He began engaging with youth programs, schools, and community centers to share his message. By connecting with the next generation of athletes, he aimed to instill a sense of awareness about mental health from an early age. He encouraged young people to embrace their emotions, seek help, and foster open conversations about mental well-being. His efforts emphasized that mental health should be prioritized alongside physical training, reinforcing that a strong mind is as crucial as a strong body.

As he continued his advocacy work, Maxx participated in community service initiatives, partnering with mental health support and awareness organizations. He participated in charity events, fundraisers, and outreach programs, dedicating time and resources to causes close to his heart. Through these initiatives, he aimed to raise awareness about the importance of mental health resources and promote access to support services for those in need. Maxx also collaborated with fellow athletes, creating a network of advocates willing to speak about their experiences and support mental health initiatives.

His efforts extended to creating content aimed at raising awareness. Maxx began producing videos, podcasts, and social media posts that tackled mental health topics head-on. He featured guests ranging from mental health professionals to fellow athletes who shared their stories. These discussions provided practical advice, coping strategies, and encouragement for those struggling with mental health issues. The content resonated with a wide audience, reinforcing that mental health is an ongoing journey requiring attention and care.

Throughout his advocacy, Maxx made it a point to emphasize the importance of self-care. He spoke openly about the tools that helped him recover, including therapy, mindfulness practices, and physical fitness. He encouraged others to explore various avenues for maintaining their mental well-being by sharing his routines and strategies. This holistic approach highlighted that mental health is multifaceted and can be nurtured through a combination of practices tailored to individual needs.

As a mental health advocate, Maxx also focused on creating supportive environments within sports organizations. He collaborated with NFL teams and leagues to promote mental health awareness and establish resources for players. By advocating for mental health days, counseling services, and open dialogue about emotional struggles, he aimed to foster an environment where athletes could seek help without fear of repercussions. This proactive stance benefited players and contributed to a cultural shift within the sports community.

Maxx's journey as a mental health advocate culminated in recognition and awards for his contributions to the field. His willingness to share his story and actively engage in advocacy earned him respect and admiration from peers, fans, and mental health professionals. He became a sought-after speaker at conferences and events focused on mental health and addiction recovery, using his platform to inspire others to speak out and seek help. His impact was felt beyond the confines of football; he became a symbol of hope for those battling mental health challenges across various communities.

In addition to his public advocacy, Maxx cultivated a strong network of support for himself. He remained connected to his recovery community, regularly attending meetings and maintaining relationships with fellow individuals in recovery. This connection provided him with the encouragement and accountability necessary for continued growth. He understood that recovery is not a solitary journey, and the bonds formed through shared experiences were invaluable.

Maxx Crosby's commitment to mental health advocacy showcases the profound influence that one individual can have on a community. By transforming his struggles into a powerful message of hope and resilience, he has created a ripple effect, inspiring countless others to confront their challenges and prioritize their mental well-being. His journey continues to evolve, and as he embraces new opportunities for growth and connection, he remains steadfast in his mission to advocate for mental health awareness and support those who need it most. Through his actions, Maxx embodies the belief that healing is possible and that we can foster understanding and compassion within our communities by sharing our stories.

Chapter 6: Leadership and Earning the Pro Bowl Spot

Embracing Leadership on and off the Field

Maxx Crosby's journey through professional football has been marked by his exceptional skills on the field and his growing leadership presence within the Raiders organization and in the broader community. As he navigated the highs and lows of his career, Crosby embraced the responsibilities of being a prominent player. He recognized that leadership extends beyond merely performing well; it involves influencing others, fostering teamwork, and advocating for positive change.

As he developed into a key player for the Raiders, Maxx understood that his actions and attitudes resonated with teammates, especially younger players looking to him for guidance. A steep learning curve characterized his early years in the NFL, but he consciously tried to absorb knowledge from veterans and coaches. Observing how established leaders conducted themselves, he began to shape his approach. Maxx realized that leadership is often about being approachable and available to listen. He took the time to connect with his teammates, ensuring they knew they could come to him with their concerns or questions. This availability established trust and built a solid foundation for collaboration.

One of the significant aspects of his leadership style was leading by example. He dedicated himself to rigorous training, demonstrating an unwavering work ethic that inspired those around him. On practice fields, Maxx consistently pushed himself to excel, whether it was during drills, scrimmages, or weight training sessions. His determination set a high-performance standard and signaled to his teammates that hard work is essential for success. This commitment became contagious; many players began to mirror his intensity, creating a culture of accountability and perseverance within the team.

Maxx's leadership extended beyond the confines of practice and games. He actively engaged in team meetings, offering constructive feedback and sharing insights based on his experiences. His willingness to speak up encouraged others to express their thoughts, fostering an environment where every player felt valued. Maxx recognized that diverse perspectives contribute to stronger decision-making and championed open dialogue within the locker room. He emphasized the importance of collaboration, urging teammates to support one another, both on and off the field.

As he embraced his leadership role, Maxx also took on mentorship responsibilities. He became a sounding board for younger players, sharing his knowledge about navigating the challenges of professional football. Understanding the pressures that rookies face, he offered advice on managing expectations, staying focused, and handling setbacks. Maxx created an inclusive atmosphere where newcomers felt comfortable asking questions and seeking guidance. This mentorship benefited the younger players and reinforced their understanding of the game, as teaching often deepens one's knowledge.

Off the field, Maxx Crosby's leadership journey took on new dimensions as he sought to give back to the community. He recognized that his platform as an NFL player could amplify important causes and inspire positive change. Motivated by his experiences, he became involved in various charitable initiatives focused on mental health awareness, youth development, and addiction recovery. By aligning his advocacy efforts with his journey, he aimed to help others navigate their challenges while reinforcing that support is crucial for growth.

Crosby's commitment to community engagement manifested in multiple ways. He organized youth camps, allowing aspiring athletes to learn from professional players. These camps emphasized skill development and the significance of teamwork, resilience, and personal growth. Maxx often shared his story, encouraging young athletes to pursue their dreams while highlighting the importance of mental well-being. His ability to connect with youth served as a reminder that leadership involves being a role model, particularly for those looking to follow in his footsteps.

Maxx's impact extended to social media, where he leveraged his presence to raise awareness about mental health and addiction recovery. He used his platform to share resources, personal stories, and motivational messages, reaching a wide audience beyond the sports community. He connected with fans who may have faced similar struggles by openly discussing his challenges and triumphs. This transparency solidified his status as a leader and positioned him as a trusted voice in conversations about mental health.

Recognizing the importance of mental health in athletics, Maxx advocated for initiatives within the NFL that prioritize players' emotional well-being. He collaborated with team officials to encourage the implementation of mental health resources and counseling services for athletes. By championing these efforts, he aimed to create an environment where players felt comfortable seeking help and discussing their challenges. Maxx's leadership in this area underscored his commitment to changing the narrative surrounding mental health, highlighting that it is a critical component of overall performance.

Throughout his journey, Maxx Crosby faced challenges that tested his resolve. Balancing the demands of professional football with personal struggles requires a level of grit that few possess. However, he leaned into his leadership role during difficult times instead of retreating. By being open about his struggles, he demonstrated vulnerability, a quality often overlooked in traditional notions of leadership. This authenticity resonated with teammates and fans, proving that strength comes in various forms.

His ability to embrace the highs and lows of his career cultivated a sense of resilience within the team. Maxx encouraged teammates to view setbacks as opportunities for growth, emphasizing that adversity can serve as a powerful teacher. This perspective became a guiding principle for many players as they navigated the challenges of a long NFL season. By promoting a mindset focused on growth and learning, he helped instill confidence in his teammates, empowering them to rise to the occasion.

As his leadership journey progressed, Maxx Crosby earned respect as a talented athlete and a dedicated leader committed to fostering a positive environment. His influence extended beyond the gridiron; he became a figure of hope and resilience for those navigating their challenges. Through his advocacy, mentorship, and unwavering dedication to personal growth, he illustrated that leadership transcends the field, impacting the lives of others in profound ways. Maxx's ability to inspire others stemmed from his genuine passion for making a difference. He understood true leadership involves a willingness to serve and uplift those around you. His contributions to his team and the community solidified his legacy as a talented football player and a transformative figure who exemplifies the best qualities of a leader. The lessons he learned throughout his journey about accountability, resilience, and the importance of mental health continue to guide him as he strives to leave a lasting impact on and off the field.

Maxx Crosby has shown that leadership is not a title but a commitment to fostering growth, understanding, and support in every endeavor. His dedication to making a positive difference in the lives of others underscores the power of influence that athletes can wield. As he continues to navigate his career, he remains a beacon of hope and strength, embodying the belief that true leadership lies in uplifting, inspiring, and connecting with others.

Career-Defining Moments Leading to Pro Bowl Selection

Maxx Crosby's path to becoming a Pro Bowl selection was marked by several pivotal moments that defined his career and solidified his reputation as one of the NFL's premier defensive talents. These moments contributed to his growth as a player and showcased his relentless pursuit of excellence. Crosby's journey reflects determination and resilience, from critical game performances to personal breakthroughs.

One of the earliest defining moments occurred during his second season in the league. After a rookie year where he showed flashes of brilliance, expectations for Crosby were higher as he entered the 2020 season. With a renewed focus on his physical conditioning and mental preparation, he came into training camp with a chip on his shoulder, eager to prove that he could consistently compete at the highest level. This sense of urgency fueled his performance during practice sessions, where he displayed an intensity that caught the attention of coaches and teammates alike. His dedication during this time signaled his readiness to take on greater challenges.

Crosby's breakout performance that season came in a primetime matchup against the New Orleans Saints. With the eyes of the football world on him, he delivered an exceptional game, recording multiple tackles and a crucial sack against the formidable offensive line. This game showcased his ability to disrupt plays and highlighted his mental fortitude. The adrenaline of performing on a big stage did not faze him; it catalyzed further growth. The way he played that night resonated with fans and analysts, marking him as a player to watch in the upcoming seasons. His efforts earned him accolades and boosted the entire defense's confidence, demonstrating they could compete with elite teams.

As the 2020 season progressed, Crosby continued to evolve. He faced significant challenges, including injuries that sidelined other key players on the defense. He stepped up as a leader instead of allowing these setbacks to discourage him. Maxx took it upon himself to mentor younger teammates, sharing insights and strategies he had learned from veterans and coaches. His leadership was crucial during tough games when the team faced formidable opponents. This willingness to adapt and take on added responsibility showcased his character and commitment to team success. His ability to remain focused and positive amidst adversity became a hallmark of his approach.

One of the career-defining moments that stood out in Crosby's journey was a critical game against the Los Angeles Chargers. He delivered a performance that left an indelible mark in a must-win situation. Crosby registered multiple sacks and made critical plays that shifted the momentum in his team's favor. It was a game that tested his skills and resolve, and he responded with poise and tenacity. The impact of this performance reverberated throughout the locker room, serving as a testament to his ability to rise to the occasion when it mattered most. His relentless pursuit of the quarterback and ability to read plays solidified his reputation as a premier pass rusher, and the league began to take notice.

As he headed into the following season, the expectations for Crosby grew. The 2021 season presented new opportunities and challenges; he was determined to make the most of them. The intensity of the competition increased, but he was ready. Crosby took his training regimen to another level, refining his technique and enhancing his physical fitness. He recognized that to be truly elite, he needed to outwork everyone around him. This dedication bore fruit early in the season, as he started to put together a string of impressive performances, quickly establishing himself as one of the most disruptive defensive players in the league.

One particular game that became a turning point in Crosby's career was against the Pittsburgh Steelers. Facing a storied franchise with a history of strong defenses, Maxx turned in a standout performance that garnered widespread acclaim. He recorded multiple tackles for loss and demonstrated a keen ability to navigate the offensive line. His relentless energy and determination were palpable throughout the game. Fans and analysts alike began to see Crosby as a promising young player and a legitimate Pro Bowl candidate. This recognition from the media and fans fueled his motivation, and he believed he could achieve greatness on the field.

Crosby's performance during the Pro Bowl voting period was spectacular. Each game leading up to the selection saw him elevate his play, showcasing an impressive combination of speed, power, and technique. The pressure of competing against some of the best talents in the NFL only seemed to energize him further. His ability to consistently create havoc in opposing backfields and his knack for making game-changing plays made him a prime candidate for selection. Each game became an opportunity to showcase his skills, and he seized those moments with fervor.

As the Pro Bowl announcement approached, the anticipation within the Raiders organization and among fans reached a fever pitch. Maxx Crosby's name had become synonymous with explosive defensive play, and many eagerly awaited his efforts' official recognition. When the announcement finally came, and he was named to the Pro Bowl, it marked a significant milestone in his career. This honor validated all the hard work, sacrifice, and perseverance he had demonstrated over the years. It was a moment that encapsulated his journey from a determined young player to an elite defensive force.

Receiving the Pro Bowl selection was not just a personal achievement for Crosby; it represented the culmination of a team effort. He understood that while individual accolades were rewarding, they were also a reflection of the collective hard work of the entire defensive unit. He took time to recognize the contributions of his teammates, emphasizing that their shared commitment to excellence played a crucial role in his success. This humility and appreciation for teamwork further solidified his standing as a leader in the locker room.

Crosby's focus remained unwavering in the days leading up to the Pro Bowl. He viewed the event as an opportunity to showcase his skills among the best players in the league and as a chance to learn from them. Engaging with fellow Pro Bowl athletes and coaches gave him valuable insights that he eagerly absorbed. Maxx embraced the opportunity to exchange ideas, techniques, and experiences with other elite players, understanding that this knowledge would only enhance his game.

The Pro Bowl was a memorable experience for Crosby, filled with excitement, camaraderie, and competitive spirit. Playing alongside the league's top talents reinforced his belief that he belonged among them. The experience motivated him to continue striving for excellence, knowing that the journey was far from over. With the recognition of his talent came a greater responsibility to perform at a high level and be a source of inspiration for younger players who looked up to him.

As Maxx Crosby reflected on his journey to the Pro Bowl, he recognized that it was filled with career-defining moments that shaped him both as a player and a person. Each performance, every challenge faced, and all the lessons learned contributed to his development. Being named to the Pro Bowl was not merely a culmination of achievements but a new beginning, igniting his passion to continue pushing boundaries and setting new standards for excellence in his career. With the support of his teammates, coaches, and the community behind him, he was determined to build on this success and make an even more significant impact in the seasons to come.

The Unrelenting Pursuit of Greatness

An unwavering commitment to greatness has characterized Maxx Crosby's journey through the NFL. From his early days as a promising talent in college football to becoming a household name in the professional league, Crosby's pursuit of excellence has driven his success. This relentless dedication stems from a combination of personal ambition, the influence of his background, and the challenges he has faced along the way.

Crosby's early life played a significant role in shaping his character. Growing up in Michigan, he was immersed in a sports-centric environment where competition was a way of life. Encouraged by his family, he developed a passion for football at a young age. His parents' support instilled a sense of resilience in him, which would prove invaluable as he navigated the ups and downs of his athletic career. The lessons he learned during these formative years, particularly the importance of hard work and perseverance, became foundational pillars in his approach to the game.

Crosby's commitment to improvement was evident throughout his college career at Eastern Michigan University. He faced numerous challenges, including proving himself against players from more prominent programs. This motivated him to enhance his skills continuously. Every practice session was an opportunity for growth, and he dedicated countless hours to refining his technique. His determination and grit did not go unnoticed. Coaches and teammates recognized his work ethic, and he quickly became a leader on and off the field. This leadership was characterized by vocal encouragement and willingness to lead by example, pushing others to elevate their game alongside him.

Crosby's determination bore fruit when he entered the NFL draft. Despite being viewed as a fourth-round pick, he carried himself with the confidence of a first-round talent. His mindset was rooted in the belief that he had something to prove. Many doubted his ability to succeed professionally, which only fueled his resolve. Crosby understood that while talent was crucial, the relentless pursuit of improvement would set him apart. This mindset propelled him through the draft process, where he focused on showcasing his skills to potential teams.

Once he secured his place in the league, the real work began. The transition from college to professional football is often challenging, with a steep learning curve that can overwhelm many young athletes. Crosby embraced this challenge enthusiastically, dedicating himself to understanding the game's intricacies. He immersed himself in film study, learning the tendencies of opposing players and offensive schemes. This level of preparation became a hallmark of his approach, allowing him to make quick adjustments during games and outmaneuver his opponents.

Maxx Crosby's rookie season was a critical phase in his career, marked by a commitment to personal and team success. He quickly earned a reputation as a tenacious pass rusher, but his journey was not without setbacks. Injuries and the physical demands of the NFL tested his resilience. Rather than allowing these obstacles to derail his progress, Crosby viewed them as opportunities for growth. Each challenge he faced became a chance to learn more about himself and the game he loved. This mental toughness and his desire to improve enabled him to make a significant impact in his first year.

The 2020 season served as a turning point in Crosby's career. With each game, he continued to build upon his established foundation, evolving into a leader on the Raiders' defense. His ability to make big plays in critical moments became a defining characteristic of his playing style. Teammates often relied on him for his skills on the field and his ability to rally the team and inspire confidence. This dual impact further solidified his status as a player who was not only talented but also possessed the qualities of a true leader.

As Crosby progressed, he faced increasing expectations. With recognition came pressure, but he viewed this as a natural part of the journey. Rather than shying away from the spotlight, he embraced it, using the attention as motivation to push himself further. His commitment to excellence remained steadfast, and he often reflected on his goals and aspirations. Each time he stepped onto the field, he carried with him the desire to succeed personally, elevate his teammates, and contribute to the team's overall success.

Pursuing greatness is often challenging, and Crosby encountered his fair share of hurdles. One of the most significant was his battle with alcoholism, a struggle that threatened to derail his promising career. This personal challenge forced him to confront difficult truths about himself and his choices' impact on his life and career. Recognizing the importance of change, he made the brave decision to seek help. Entering rehab was not just a necessary step but a pivotal moment in his life. This journey toward sobriety allowed him to reclaim his focus and dedication to football, reigniting his passion for the game. Emerging from rehab, Crosby was a changed man and a more determined player. The experience equipped him with a newfound perspective on life, fueling his ambition to make the most of every opportunity. He committed to a lifestyle prioritizing his mental and physical health, understanding that both were essential to achieving greatness. His story became an inspiration not just for his teammates but for countless fans who admired his resilience and willingness to confront his demons.

As Crosby continued to thrive in the NFL, he made it his mission to advocate for mental health awareness. His journey highlighted the importance of addressing mental health issues, particularly in the high-pressure environment of professional sports. By sharing his story, he aimed to create a supportive community where athletes could openly discuss their struggles and seek help without fear of judgment. This commitment to advocacy became another facet of his pursuit of greatness, as he realized that true success transcends personal achievements.

In the subsequent seasons, Crosby solidified his status as a key player for the Raiders. His relentless pursuit of excellence resonated throughout the team, inspiring others to strive for greatness. He became known not only for his on-field prowess but also for his leadership qualities. Teammates looked up to him as a source of motivation and strength, and his willingness to put in the hard work set a standard for others to follow. This leadership extended beyond the gridiron; Crosby took the time to mentor younger players, sharing insights and encouraging them to pursue their dreams with the same enthusiasm that had propelled him.

Crosby's journey is a testament to the idea that greatness is not merely about talent or accolades but the relentless pursuit of improvement and the willingness to overcome obstacles. His story reflects a dedication to achieving personal success and lifting others. Each game, every practice, and every challenge became an opportunity for growth, allowing him to refine his craft and elevate those around him. As he continues navigating his career, the commitment to greatness remains a central theme in Maxx Crosby's life, driving him forward and inspiring countless others to pursue their paths with unwavering determination.

Chapter 7: Signature Playing Style and Defensive Prowess

High Motor and Relentless Effort

Maxx Crosby is renowned for his exceptional work ethic and the relentless energy he brings to every game. His high motor is a defining characteristic that sets him apart from many players in the league. While talent is undoubtedly essential, his unyielding effort and passion for the game make him a standout player. This unwavering commitment is reflected in his performance on the field and his preparation and approach to each season.

Crosby's enthusiasm for the game was evident from the outset of his career. He approaches every play with an intensity that resonates with teammates and coaches alike. This energy is contagious; it motivates those around him to elevate their performance. Crosby's relentless pursuit often results in game-changing moments, whether rushing the quarterback, chasing down ball carriers, or pursuing the play down the field. His ability to maintain high effort throughout a game has made him a player for which opposing offenses must constantly account.

Crosby's work ethic is deeply ingrained in his character. Growing up, he learned the value of hard work from his family, who emphasized the importance of effort in achieving one's goals. This lesson stayed with him as he navigated his youth football career, facing obstacles and challenges. Instead of allowing setbacks to deter him, he used them as fuel to drive himself harder. This foundation of perseverance laid the groundwork for his future success, fostering a mentality that would carry him through the competitive landscape of college football and into the NFL.

His time at Eastern Michigan University was pivotal in honing this relentless approach. Crosby was not the most heralded player entering college, often overlooked by larger programs. Rather than succumbing to doubt, he took it as an opportunity to prove himself. His practices were characterized by intense effort, and he quickly became a player willing to outwork his competition. This relentless attitude caught the attention of his coaches, who recognized his potential and dedicated themselves to helping him refine his skills. They encouraged him to embrace his physicality and enhance his technique, knowing that his work ethic would complement his growing talent.

As Crosby transitioned to the NFL, the level of competition intensified, but his high motor remained a constant. The rigors of professional football tested his stamina and determination, but he adapted by focusing on his conditioning and preparation. Understanding the demands of an NFL season, he dedicated time to fitness and recovery, ensuring that he could maintain his energy levels week in and week out. His performance reflected this commitment, as he consistently ranked among the top players in hustle stats, indicating his ability to make plays even in critical moments.

During games, Crosby's relentless effort is on full display. He plays aggressively, showcasing his physicality and willingness to engage opponents. His high motor allows him to press through fatigue, making him a formidable presence on the field. There are moments when other players might take a play off or become complacent, but Crosby's drive never wanes. This tenacity has earned him the respect of his teammates and made him a nightmare for offensive linemen tasked with blocking him.

Crosby's ability to maintain his energy level even in the most challenging situations is a testament to his mental fortitude. He thrives in high-pressure scenarios, often stepping up when his team needs him most. This resilience stems from a deep understanding of the game and a profound love for football. Each snap is an opportunity for him to impact the game positively, and he approaches this responsibility with a sense of urgency. His tenacity can lead to critical tackles, sacks, or forced fumbles that change the momentum of a game, showcasing how vital relentless effort can be in high-stakes situations.

The impact of Crosby's high motor extends beyond individual plays; it influences the entire defense. His relentless pursuit of excellence inspires teammates to match his intensity, fostering a culture of hard work and commitment within the Raiders' locker room. Veteran players and rookies look to him as a role model, seeing firsthand how effort and determination can lead to success. This leadership by example has helped cultivate a cohesive unit that rallies around a shared goal, continuously pushing each other to improve.

Coaches and analysts often highlight the importance of a player's motor when evaluating talent. While natural ability is a crucial aspect of success in the NFL, it is often the players who possess an insatiable drive who make the most significant impact. Crosby embodies this philosophy, showcasing how hard work and effort can elevate a player's game. His performances serve as a reminder that even in a league filled with elite athletes, those willing to put in the extra work often stand out.

In addition to his physical contributions, Crosby's high motor skills also translate into mental advantages. His relentless effort often forces opposing teams to adjust their strategies to account for his presence on the field. Offenses must plan around his explosiveness, often leading to double teams or adjustments in blocking schemes. This focus on Crosby can create opportunities for his teammates, allowing them to thrive and make plays. The ripple effect of his hard work illustrates how one player's dedication can elevate an entire unit.

Crosby's journey is a testament to the power of effort and determination in sports. His relentless pursuit of greatness serves as an inspiration to aspiring athletes everywhere. By embodying the principles of hard work and perseverance, he demonstrates that success is achievable through dedication and a commitment to improving every day. As he continues to carve out his legacy in the NFL, his high motor and relentless effort will undoubtedly remain integral components of his identity as a player and a leader.

This approach extends beyond the football field and permeates his life. Crosby recognizes that the lessons learned through sports can be applied to various endeavors, from personal challenges to professional ambitions. The discipline and focus he cultivated through football empower him to face obstacles head-on, whether in his career or personal life. His commitment to continuous improvement serves as a reminder that effort is a key ingredient in any success story.

As Maxx Crosby looks ahead to the future, he remains focused on maintaining his high motor and relentless effort. His commitment to the game and his teammates is unwavering, ensuring he will remain a force in the league. By embodying the principles of hard work and determination, Crosby sets a standard for others to follow, inspiring the next generation of athletes to pursue their dreams with the same intensity and passion he has demonstrated throughout his career. His relentless spirit will undoubtedly shine through every challenge and triumph, impacting the football game and those who love it.

Mastering the Art of Sacking Quarterbacks

Maxx Crosby has established himself as one of the most formidable pass rushers in the NFL, known for his uncanny ability to sack quarterbacks. Mastering the art of sacking requires natural talent and a combination of technique, strategy, and relentless determination. For Crosby, this mastery has been honed through years of dedication, resulting in a skill set that makes him a constant threat on the field.

Crosby demonstrated an innate understanding of the game from playing football early on. This understanding became particularly evident as he progressed through high school and college, where he began to refine his skills as a pass rusher. While at Eastern Michigan University, he developed a reputation for his explosive first step and ability to bend around the edge. Coaches and teammates noted how his physical attributes and strong work ethic made him a player to watch. He spent countless hours studying film, analyzing his technique and the tendencies of opposing quarterbacks and offensive linemen.

Understanding the mechanics of quarterback play became crucial for Crosby as he sought to exploit weaknesses. He immersed himself in learning about different offensive schemes, focusing on how quarterbacks would drop back and the timing involved in their throws. This knowledge allowed him to anticipate their movements, positioning himself to create disruptive plays. His ability to read the game and make quick decisions became one of his standout traits, setting him apart from many of his peers.

Crosby's technique is a blend of speed, strength, and finesse. While many pass rushers rely solely on brute force to overpower offensive linemen, Crosby employs a variety of moves to keep his opponents guessing. He has mastered the use of swim moves, spin moves, and powerful bull rushes, allowing him to adapt his approach based on the situation. Each technique requires precise timing and execution, which he has perfected through relentless practice and a commitment to his craft. His repertoire of pass-rushing moves keeps offensive linemen on high alert, making it challenging for them to predict his next move.

One of the keys to Crosby's success as a sack artist is his relentless pursuit of the quarterback. His high motor skills enable him to maintain impressive energy throughout the game, allowing him to chase down plays that other defenders might give up on. This determination leads to sacks and forces quarterbacks to make hurried throws or retreat from the pocket. It creates a ripple effect, disrupting the offensive rhythm and opening up opportunities for his teammates to capitalize on mistakes.

Timing is another crucial factor in Crosby's ability to sack quarterbacks effectively. He has an instinct for when to engage offensive linemen and when to disengage to make a play on the quarterback. This timing is essential during passing downs, where the window for success is often limited. Crosby's quick first step gives him an advantage, allowing him to explode off the line and close the gap between himself and the quarterback. His ability to time his rush with the snap of the ball gives him a crucial edge in one-on-one situations.

As a pass rusher, Crosby also understands the importance of leverage. He can gain an advantage over larger offensive linemen by utilizing his body positioning. He uses angles effectively, working to position himself in a way that allows him to exploit any openings. This attention to detail in leveraging his body enhances his ability to sack the quarterback and helps him defend against runs. His understanding of leverage allows him to maintain balance and power, making him a versatile defender capable of impacting the game in multiple ways.

Crosby's effectiveness is not solely due to his physical attributes and technical prowess; it is also a product of his mental approach to the game. He has a deep-seated desire to continually improve, always seeking ways to refine his craft. This drive manifests in his preparation for each game, where he spends hours studying film, analyzing opponents, and developing game plans tailored to exploit weaknesses. He engages with coaches to gain insights into different offensive strategies, enhancing his understanding of approaching each matchup. This meticulous preparation ensures that he enters every game with a comprehensive understanding of what to expect, positioning himself to maximize his effectiveness.

Crosby's ability to sack quarterbacks has not gone unnoticed. As he continues to build on his early successes, he has drawn attention from fans, analysts, and players alike. His growing reputation as a premier pass rusher has increased scrutiny from opposing offenses, which have started implementing strategies to counter his influence. This has not deterred him; instead, he views it as a challenge that fuels his desire to elevate his game further. He thrives on the competition, using attention to motivate himself to adapt and innovate his approach.

Another aspect of mastering the art of sacking is the importance of teamwork. While individual efforts are essential, successful pass-rushing often involves synergy with teammates. Crosby understands that he is part of a larger defensive unit, and his effectiveness is magnified when he works with others. He communicates with his fellow defenders, ensuring they are all on the same page regarding pass-rushing techniques and stunts. This collaboration creates confusion for offensive linemen, allowing Crosby to exploit gaps and opportunities that may go unnoticed.

Crosby's journey to mastering the art of sacking quarterbacks is also a testament to his resilience. He has faced challenges throughout his career, including injuries and tough matchups. However, his unwavering determination has allowed him to overcome obstacles and continue to improve. Each setback has taught him valuable lessons, reinforcing the importance of adaptability and growth. Rather than being discouraged by adversity, Crosby uses it to motivate himself further, ensuring he remains a player in the league.

As he looks to the future, Crosby is committed to maintaining his status as one of the elite pass rushers in the NFL. He recognizes the fierce competition, and each season brings new challenges. He aims to solidify his legacy with every sack while inspiring a new generation of defenders. His relentless pursuit of excellence serves as a reminder that mastery in football is not solely about physical talent; it is a combination of preparation, technique, and an unwavering commitment to improvement.

Maxx Crosby's journey in mastering the art of sacking quarterbacks embodies the principles of hard work, determination, and skill. His relentless pursuit of excellence and refusal to settle for mediocrity has solidified his position as one of the premier pass rushers in the league. As he continues to refine his craft and adapt to the ever-evolving nature of the game, his legacy as a dynamic and impactful player will undoubtedly continue to grow, inspiring both current and future generations of athletes. His journey highlights that the art of sacking quarterbacks can be mastered with the right mindset and dedication, profoundly impacting the game of football.

Impact on the Raiders' Defensive Line

Maxx Crosby's arrival on the Oakland Raiders defensive line marked a transformative phase for the team, characterized by a surge in performance and a new identity. His tenacity, skill set, and relentless work ethic significantly reshaped the defensive front, influencing not just his performance but also that of his teammates and the overall defensive strategy employed by the coaching staff.

Crosby's impact on the Raiders began as soon as he stepped onto the practice field. His energy was infectious, sparking renewed motivation among his fellow defenders. Known for his tireless approach to practice, he consistently pushed himself and others around him to elevate their games. Teammates quickly noticed his willingness to put in the extra hours, whether it was refining technique or studying film. This commitment instilled a sense of accountability within the unit, creating a culture where hard work was encouraged and expected.

His playing style brought a dynamic element to the Raiders' defensive line. Crosby is distinguished by his explosive speed and agility, which allow him to easily navigate around offensive linemen. This unique combination of attributes makes him a constant threat, capable of disrupting plays in the backfield and at the line of scrimmage. His ability to pressure quarterbacks created opportunities for himself and opened avenues for his fellow defensive linemen and linebackers. The attention he garnered from opposing offenses often resulted in favorable matchups for his teammates, amplifying the effectiveness of the entire defensive line. One of the key aspects of Crosby's impact lies in his ability to consistently generate sacks and quarterback pressures. His performance elevated the Raiders' defensive line into a more aggressive unit, one that was feared by opposing quarterbacks. The presence of a dominant pass rusher like Crosby forced offenses to adjust their game plans, often leading to quicker throws or the utilization of additional blockers in an attempt to neutralize him. This shift in focus from opposing offenses gave the Raiders advantages, enhancing their defensive strategy.

His work against the run complemented the effectiveness of Crosby's pass rush. He developed a reputation for being a versatile defender capable of making plays on all fronts. His keen awareness of offensive schemes allowed him to read plays effectively, enabling him to recognize run designs early and make decisive moves to thwart them. His ability to set the edge on running plays added a layer of strength to the Raiders' defensive line, ensuring that opposing teams faced a formidable challenge on both passing and running downs.

Crosby's success also inspired his teammates to reach new heights. As he consistently displayed exceptional performance on the field, other players within the defensive line began to follow suit. The competition within the unit intensified, with players striving to match Crosby's level of excellence. This collective improvement was evident in the overall performance of the Raiders' defense, which began to show marked progress in key areas. Crosby's influence fostered a sense of camaraderie among his teammates as they worked together to achieve shared goals.

Additionally, Crosby's leadership qualities became increasingly apparent as he matured within the organization. He emerged not only as a standout player but also as a vocal leader on the defensive line. His willingness to share insights and knowledge with younger players was crucial to their development. Crosby's approachability allowed teammates to seek guidance, fostering an environment where questions were welcomed, and learning was encouraged. This mentorship aspect contributed significantly to the growth of the Raiders' defensive front, as younger players benefited from his experience and expertise.

As the season progressed, Crosby's impact became even more pronounced. He consistently found ways to make crucial plays at pivotal moments, demonstrating an ability to rise to the occasion. Whether it was a game-changing sack or a key stop on third down, his performance often provided the spark needed to energize the entire team. This knack for making impactful plays highlighted his talent and reinforced his role as a linchpin within the Raiders' defensive strategy.

Crosby's influence extended beyond the field, as he became a community figure and ambassador for the Raiders. His dedication to his craft and the values he embodied resonated with fans and players alike. He engaged with the community, participating in events and initiatives to inspire and uplift others. This connection to the community fostered a sense of pride among fans. It reinforced the notion that the Raiders were not just a football team but a family representing a shared identity.

The Raiders coaching staff recognized the profound effect Crosby had on the defensive line, and they began to tailor their game plans to maximize his strengths. Defensive coordinators employed various schemes designed to free him up and create opportunities for disruption. Implementing stunts and blitz packages showcased Crosby's versatility and ability to excel in different situations. This strategic adaptation highlighted his integral role in the defense and underscored the coaching staff's belief in his capabilities.

Crosby's journey in the NFL was marked by an evolution in his game and role within the team. He embraced challenges and faced adversity head-on, demonstrating a resilience that resonated throughout the locker room. His ability to navigate the ups and downs of the league became a source of inspiration for his teammates, showcasing the importance of perseverance in achieving success. This mental fortitude complemented his physical prowess, reinforcing that true greatness involves talent and a relentless spirit. The Raider's defensive line thrived under his influence as Crosby continued to develop as a player. The cohesion within the unit improved, allowing it to function as a well-oiled machine capable of executing complex defensive strategies. This synergy translated into on-field success as the team began to achieve critical victories that showcased their growth. Crosby's contributions were integral to elevating the defense's performance, leading to a reputation as a formidable force within the league.

Looking forward, Crosby's impact on the Raiders' defensive line signifies a new era for the team. His presence has not only raised the performance of individual players but has also contributed to a culture of excellence within the organization. The Raiders' commitment to building a championship-caliber team is reflected in their investment in players like Crosby, who embody the tenacity and skill required to succeed at the highest level. As the team continues to evolve, Crosby remains a key figure in their journey, embodying the resilience and determination that define the Raiders' identity. His legacy as a transformative player will continue to resonate throughout the organization for years to come, inspiring future generations of athletes who aspire to make their mark on the game.

Chapter 8: Maxx Crosby's Impact on the Las Vegas Raiders

Becoming a Pillar of the Raiders' Defense

Maxx Crosby's evolution into a pillar of the Raiders' defense reflects a journey marked by dedication, hard work, and a relentless pursuit of excellence. His rise within the organization is a testament to his natural talent and significant effort in honing his skills and building relationships with teammates and coaches. This commitment has positioned him as a central figure in the defensive scheme, whose influence extends beyond mere statistics.

When he entered the league, Crosby demonstrated an insatiable desire to improve. Early on, he recognized that success in the NFL required raw ability, a strong work ethic, and a willingness to learn. His days in practice were characterized by palpable intensity as he pushed himself and his fellow defenders to elevate their performance. This work ethic soon became contagious, as his passion for the game inspired those around him to adopt a similar mindset.

Crosby's impact on the field was felt immediately as he brought a unique combination of speed and agility, making him a nightmare for opposing quarterbacks. His ability to explode off the line of scrimmage, combined with his relentless motor, allowed him to disrupt plays at critical moments. This consistency made him a formidable force in the trenches and instilled confidence in his teammates, who knew they could rely on him to make crucial plays when it mattered most.

As his career progressed, Crosby's role expanded, and he began to embrace the responsibilities of being a leader on the defense. His growth as a player coincided with his evolution into a mentor for younger teammates. He recognized the importance of sharing knowledge and experience with the next generation, fostering a culture of learning and improvement within the defensive unit. This approach helped create a sense of unity, allowing players to develop camaraderie and work collaboratively towards common goals.

Crosby's ability to communicate effectively with his teammates and coaching staff further solidified his leadership position. He actively engaged in discussions during team meetings and practice sessions, providing insights and perspectives that often led to improved strategies on the field. His willingness to speak up and offer suggestions demonstrated his investment in the team's success and showcased his understanding of the game at a high level. This open line of communication contributed to a more cohesive and adaptable defense.

Moreover, Crosby's resilience in facing challenges set a powerful example for his peers. The NFL is known for its physically and mentally demanding nature, and players are often tested by adversity. Crosby faced his share of obstacles, including injuries and the pressure to perform consistently at a high level. Instead of allowing these challenges to define him, he used them as motivation to push harder and improve. His ability to bounce back from setbacks resonated with teammates, reinforcing that perseverance is key to success in the league.

Crosby's on-field performance did not go unnoticed, as his statistics began to reflect his impact. He became known for his ability to sack quarterbacks and his skill in tackling ball carriers, reading plays, and making critical stops. His versatility allowed the coaching staff to deploy him in various roles within the defense, maximizing his strengths and adapting to the team's needs. This adaptability showcased his intelligence as a player and further established his value as an essential component of the Raiders' defensive strategy.

The emotional and mental aspects of the game also played a significant role in Crosby's development. He understood that football is as much a mental game as physical. He studied opponents, analyzed game films, and prepared for offensive schemes. This commitment to preparation allowed him to anticipate plays and make quicker decisions on the field, resulting in more impactful performances. His ability to stay mentally sharp under pressure distinguished him as a top-tier player and bolstered his reputation as a key defensive asset.

As the seasons progressed, Crosby's influence became even more apparent during crucial games. He had a knack for stepping up in high-pressure situations, whether a key third down or a late-game scenario where the team needed a defensive stop. His knack for making plays when they mattered most solidified his status as a go-to player on the defense, earning him the trust of both coaches and teammates. This trust was evident in how the defensive scheme evolved to leverage his strengths, allowing him to shine in moments that defined games.

Crosby's community engagement and commitment to positively impacting off the field further enhanced his role as a pillar of the Raiders' defense. He recognized that being a professional athlete came with a platform that could be used to inspire and uplift others. By participating in community events and initiatives, he forged connections with fans and local organizations, demonstrating that he was invested in more than just football. This dedication to service reinforced his status as a role model and allowed him to leave a lasting impact beyond the gridiron.

His involvement in mental health advocacy showcased another dimension of his leadership. Crosby openly discussed his struggles and the importance of mental well-being, encouraging teammates to prioritize their mental health. By fostering a supportive environment, he not only helped to destigmatize mental health issues within the sport but also created a culture where players felt comfortable seeking help and discussing their challenges. This aspect of his leadership resonated deeply with many, further solidifying his standing as a respected figure in the locker room.

As Crosby continued performing at an elite level, he garnered recognition from fans, the media, and the league. His selection to the Pro Bowl was a testament to his hard work and dedication, marking a significant milestone in his career. This recognition was not solely about individual accolades; it underscored his contribution to the team's success and his pivotal role in elevating the defensive unit.

Crosby's trajectory suggests that he will continue to be a cornerstone of the Raiders' defense for years. His combination of talent, work ethic, and leadership qualities sets a standard for excellence that will resonate throughout the organization. As the team builds toward future success, Crosby's influence will undoubtedly play a vital role in shaping the next generation of Raiders players. His journey from a rookie with potential to a key pillar of the defense serves as an inspiring narrative, illustrating the power of perseverance, dedication, and a commitment to greatness.

Crosby embodies the ethos of the Raiders organization, a franchise with a rich history and a tradition of resilience. His commitment to the team, both on and off the field, solidifies his legacy as a player who excelled individually and elevated those around him. As he continues to build on his successes, his impact will echo throughout the Raiders' history, inspiring future players to strive for excellence and embrace the principles of hard work, teamwork, and leadership that Crosby exemplifies.

Building a Legacy in Las Vegas

Maxx Crosby's journey in the NFL has been more than just a series of impressive stats and accolades; it has evolved into a significant legacy within the Las Vegas Raiders organization. Since joining the Raiders, Crosby has showcased his talent on the field and embraced the responsibilities of being a prominent figure in a franchise that recently transitioned to a new city. His commitment to excellence as a player and leader forged a deep connection with the community and set the stage for a legacy transcending mere performance.

Arriving in Las Vegas during a transition period for the franchise, Crosby recognized the unique opportunity presented to him and his teammates. The move to a new city meant a fresh start, and it was imperative to establish a strong identity and culture. He took it upon himself to become a catalyst for this transformation, embodying the fierce spirit that the Raiders have long been known for. With determination and passion, Crosby sought to create a defensive unit to compete at the highest level and inspire the fans who had embraced the team.

Crosby's style of play immediately resonated with the Las Vegas fanbase. His high-energy performances, characterized by relentless pursuit and a never-give-up attitude, struck a chord with supporters who appreciate hard work and dedication. Each tackle, sack, and forced fumble became a testament to his commitment to the game and his desire to make an impact. As fans flocked to Allegiant Stadium, they witnessed a player who exemplified the Raider spirit, who played not just for himself but for the badge on his chest and the city that welcomed him.

The importance of community engagement cannot be overstated in building a legacy. Crosby embraced his role as a community ambassador, recognizing that the relationship between the team and its fans extends beyond game day. He actively participated in local events, youth initiatives, and charitable efforts, understanding that connecting with the community is vital to establishing a lasting legacy. By engaging with fans and sharing his personal story, Crosby fostered a sense of belonging and loyalty, transforming casual supporters into passionate advocates for the team.

Crosby's efforts to give back to the community reflect a broader commitment to social responsibility, which has become increasingly significant in professional sports. He championed various causes, particularly those related to mental health and wellness, leveraging his platform to raise awareness and promote open dialogue. His authenticity in addressing these issues resonated deeply with fans inspired by his willingness to share his struggles and triumphs. This genuine connection forged an emotional bond between Crosby and the community, positioning him as a role model for aspiring athletes and fans.

As Crosby's career progressed, his influence within the Raiders organization grew. He became a pivotal player on the field and assumed a mentorship role for younger teammates. His willingness to share knowledge, provide guidance, and cultivate a culture of accountability elevated the entire defensive unit. By fostering an environment where players felt empowered to learn and improve, Crosby contributed to the team's overall success. This leadership extended beyond tactical discussions; it encompassed the importance of hard work, discipline, and resilience, qualities that defined the Raiders' ethos.

The on-field success that Crosby experienced was a natural byproduct of his commitment to excellence. His ability to consistently perform at a high level garnered respect from coaches, teammates, and opponents. He became a cornerstone of the Raiders' defense, known for his ability to disrupt plays and make crucial stops at pivotal moments. This level of performance solidified his place within the team and increased his visibility within the league. As accolades and recognition followed, Crosby understood that each achievement contributed to the broader narrative of his legacy in Las Vegas.

However, Crosby's legacy is not solely defined by individual achievements or statistics. It encompasses his impact on the Raiders' identity as they established themselves in a new city. His commitment to the team and the community helped shape a culture that resonates with Las Vegas, a city known for its resilience and passion. Crosby's presence became synonymous with the franchise's growth and evolution as the Raiders embraced their new home. He represented not only the aspirations of the team but also the spirit of a city that welcomed them with open arms.

The significance of building a legacy is often measured by the ability to inspire others. Crosby's journey from a rookie to a leader exemplifies the power of perseverance and dedication. His story is a beacon of hope for young athletes dreaming of making it in professional sports. By overcoming obstacles, demonstrating resilience, and remaining committed to his craft, Crosby has shown that greatness is achievable with hard work and determination. His legacy in Las Vegas will undoubtedly inspire future generations to strive for their success, both on and off the field.

As the Raiders continue to carve out their identity in Las Vegas, Crosby's influence will remain a defining aspect of the franchise's history. He is not just a player who donned the silver and black; he symbolizes hope, resilience, and dedication. His commitment to the community and the franchise exemplifies the Raiders' ideals for unity, strength, and a relentless pursuit of excellence.

Looking to the future, the potential for Crosby's legacy to expand is immense. As he continues to perform at a high level and serve as a leader within the organization, his impact will echo through the annals of Raiders history. His role as a community advocate, mentor, and on-field leader ensures his influence will be felt for years. The bond he has forged with fans, teammates, and the city of Las Vegas will remain a significant part of the Raiders' story, a narrative of a player who embraced the challenge of building a legacy in a new home.

In the grand tapestry of NFL history, Maxx Crosby's journey serves as a reminder that true greatness extends beyond personal achievements. It is about the connections forged, the lives touched, and the positive impact left on the community. As he continues to pursue excellence, Crosby embodies what it means to be a Raider, a player who excels on the field and strives to uplift those around him, leaving a lasting legacy that will resonate through generations.

Creating an Identity in the Silver and Black

Creating a strong identity is crucial for any sports franchise, and for the Las Vegas Raiders, this journey began anew when they moved significantly from Oakland to Sin City. Maxx Crosby was among the players who embraced this challenge wholeheartedly. His contributions went beyond personal accolades and performances; they played an essential role in shaping the team's identity within a new environment. As the Raiders sought to establish their presence in Las Vegas, Crosby emerged as a driving force, embodying the spirit and resilience associated with the franchise.

From the outset, Crosby's arrival in Las Vegas was marked by a determination to uphold the storied legacy of the Raiders while simultaneously infusing his energy and passion into the team. He understood that the franchise's history is rich and complex, steeped in a culture that values toughness, grit, and an unwavering commitment to excellence. This understanding motivated him to immerse himself in the values the Raiders represent, striving to become a symbol of what it means to don the iconic silver and black. Crosby's approach to establishing an identity began with his relentless work ethic. He quickly became known for his dedication to practice and preparation. Every workout, training session, and game was an opportunity to showcase his talent and commitment to the team's success. This approach resonated with his teammates, who recognized Crosby as a player willing to put in the effort required to elevate the team's collective performance. His work ethic became contagious, fostering a culture of accountability and determination throughout the locker room.

His willingness to lead by example further strengthened the connection between Crosby and his teammates. He didn't shy away from the pressure of being a prominent figure in the Raiders' defensive lineup. Instead, he embraced it. During crucial games, he would rally his fellow players, encouraging them to rise and execute at the highest level. This instinctive leadership helped galvanize the defense, instilling confidence that enabled them to perform under pressure. It became evident that Crosby was focused on individual glory and the team's collective success.

As the Raiders established their new home in Las Vegas, they faced the challenge of creating a fan base that resonated with the community. Crosby played a pivotal role in this endeavor, as he made a concerted effort to engage with fans, acknowledging the significance of their support. Whether attending community events or participating in charity initiatives, Crosby recognized the importance of building relationships beyond the football field. This connection with the fans created a sense of unity, establishing the foundation of the Raiders' identity as a team that competes fiercely and stands as a community pillar.

Crosby's charisma and authenticity contributed to the Raiders' identity as a franchise deeply rooted in the values of loyalty and resilience. Fans began to see him as more than just a player; he became a representative of the Raider Nation. His passionate style of play and genuine connection with supporters helped to cultivate a culture that encouraged fans to rally behind the team. This relationship was vital in creating an authentic and relatable identity that resonated with the aspirations and hopes of the Las Vegas community.

The impact of their unique brand further enhanced the significance of the Raiders' identity. The silver and black color scheme and the iconic pirate logo represent the team's history and commitment to being bold and daring. Crosby embodied this ethos, wearing the colors with pride and representing the spirit of a franchise that has weathered challenges and celebrated triumphs. His presence on the field became synonymous with the identity of the Raiders, reinforcing the idea that this was a team built on a foundation of courage and determination.

As Crosby continued to perform at a high level, his evolution as a player mirrored the Raiders' journey to establish their identity in Las Vegas. He developed into a leader on and off the field, fostering a culture of excellence reflected in the team's performances. His ability to disrupt opposing offenses and make game-changing plays served as a beacon of hope for fans, reinforcing the idea that the Raiders were a force to be reckoned with. Each success added layers to the team's identity, making it clear that the franchise was not merely a newcomer but a contender.

Throughout this process, Crosby became more than just a representative of the Raiders; he became an advocate for Las Vegas. The community embraced the team, and Crosby took the initiative to show his appreciation. His involvement in charitable events and outreach programs allowed him to connect with residents personally. By championing causes that mattered to the community, he exemplified the values of compassion and commitment, reinforcing the notion that the Raiders were not just a team playing for wins but a franchise that cared deeply about the people it represented.

A spirit of resilience and defiance characterizes the identity of the Raiders, and Crosby personified these traits. He overcame personal challenges and setbacks, using them to motivate himself further. His journey through adversity mirrored the franchise's struggles, making him a relatable figure for fans who may have faced their hardships. This connection added depth to the Raiders' identity, creating a narrative that extended beyond the field and resonated with the life experiences of the community.

As the Raiders continue to navigate their new landscape in Las Vegas, Crosby's role in shaping their identity remains pivotal. He has established himself as a key figure whose contributions go beyond statistics and accolades. His impact is woven into the franchise's fabric, serving as a reminder of what it means to embody the Raider spirit. His relentless pursuit of greatness, commitment to the community, and ability to inspire those around him will define the Raiders' identity for years to come.

The legacy Crosby is building in Las Vegas is not solely about personal achievements but about creating a lasting impact on a franchise that is redefining itself in a new city. As he continues to play an integral role in the team's evolution, the values he represents will resonate throughout the organization and the community. The Raiders are not just a team but a symbol of hope, resilience, and unity. With players like Maxx Crosby at the forefront, the franchise's identity is firmly rooted in the spirit of Las Vegas and the loyalty of its fans, creating a powerful narrative that will endure for generations.

Chapter 9: Off the Field: Charity, Advocacy, and Giving Back

Advocating for Addiction Recovery and Mental Health Awareness

Advocating for addiction recovery and mental health awareness has become a critical focus for many individuals who have faced personal challenges, and Maxx Crosby stands out as a notable figure in this important movement. Having navigated his struggles with addiction, Crosby has transformed his experiences into a platform for change, emphasizing the necessity of dialogue around these often-stigmatized issues. His journey reflects not just a personal battle but also a commitment to shedding light on the broader societal impacts of addiction and mental health.

Crosby's story of addiction is not uncommon in the world of sports, where pressure and expectations can lead to unhealthy coping mechanisms. However, his willingness to speak openly about these struggles sets him apart. By sharing his experiences, he has encouraged others to acknowledge their challenges and seek help, breaking down the barriers that often prevent individuals from addressing their mental health. This candid approach has resonated deeply within the sports community and beyond, allowing fans and fellow athletes to see a different perspective on vulnerability and strength.

His advocacy efforts began to take shape when he realized that silence surrounding mental health and addiction only perpetuates stigma and isolation. Crosby has consistently utilized social media platforms to reach a wider audience, sharing messages of hope and support. His posts often emphasize the importance of acknowledging one's struggles and taking proactive steps toward recovery. Through his transparency, he has fostered an environment where individuals feel empowered to speak out, creating a ripple effect beyond the confines of the football field.

Crosby's commitment to addiction recovery goes hand in hand with his desire to promote mental health awareness. He has collaborated with various organizations focusing on these issues, participating in campaigns to provide resources and support for needy individuals. By aligning himself with these initiatives, he amplifies their message and broadens their reach. His involvement is not merely symbolic; he actively engages with these organizations, often sharing his story at events and fundraisers, highlighting the necessity of community support in the recovery journey.

One of the pivotal aspects of Crosby's advocacy is his emphasis on the role of community in the recovery process. He understands that overcoming addiction is rarely a solitary endeavor; it requires a network of support, understanding, and encouragement. Crosby frequently speaks about the importance of surrounding oneself with positive influences and the critical role of family, friends, and teammates in fostering an environment conducive to healing. This message resonates particularly with young athletes who may feel isolated in their struggles, reminding them they are not alone in their battles.

Crosby has also used his platform to emphasize the significance of mental health resources in sports. He recognizes that athletes are often subject to immense pressure, leading many to grapple with anxiety, depression, and other mental health issues. By advocating for the availability of mental health resources within professional sports, he is pushing for systemic change that prioritizes the well-being of athletes. His advocacy has sparked conversations within the NFL and other sports leagues, urging organizations to recognize the necessity of mental health support as an integral part of player development and care.

In addition to his public advocacy, Crosby's journey provides a compelling narrative that highlights the realities of addiction and recovery. He candidly discusses his challenges during his darkest moments, emphasizing that recovery is not linear. His honesty about relapses and setbacks underscores the complexity of addiction, illustrating that the journey toward recovery requires patience, resilience, and an unwavering commitment to self-improvement. By normalizing these experiences, he creates a sense of relatability for those who may feel ashamed of their struggles, fostering a culture of understanding and acceptance.

Crosby's impact extends beyond the confines of the football field. He has become a beacon of hope for many individuals battling addiction, showing that recovery is possible and that it is okay to seek help. His messages of resilience and empowerment resonate with audiences of all backgrounds, proving that mental health awareness is a universal concern that transcends socio-economic barriers. Through speaking engagements and community outreach, Crosby inspires countless individuals to take charge of their mental health, encouraging them to prioritize their well-being and seek the support they need.

Moreover, Crosby's advocacy highlights the need for broader societal change in how addiction and mental health are perceived. By challenging the stereotypes and misconceptions surrounding these issues, he plays a crucial role in shifting the narrative toward a more compassionate understanding of many's struggles. His efforts contribute to a growing movement that seeks to eliminate stigma and promote empathy, fostering an environment where individuals feel safe to discuss their mental health without fear of judgment.

Crosby's commitment to addiction recovery and mental health awareness also serves as a reminder of the importance of education and resources. He advocates for increased access to mental health services, emphasizing that everyone should have the opportunity to seek help regardless of their circumstances. By championing initiatives that provide mental health and addiction education, he empowers individuals to make informed decisions about their well-being, equipping them with the tools necessary to navigate their journeys.

As he continues to navigate his path to recovery, Crosby remains dedicated to advocating for others. His story is a powerful reminder that the journey is ongoing and that it is possible to transform personal struggles into a force for good. His resilience and determination to make a difference have solidified his role as an influential figure in the movement for addiction recovery and mental health awareness.

Crosby's advocacy highlights the interconnectedness of addiction recovery, mental health, and community support. He emphasizes that healing is a collective effort, requiring understanding and compassion from all corners of society. His message resonates deeply, encouraging individuals to look beyond their own experiences and consider the broader impact of their actions on those around them. By fostering a sense of community and support, he cultivates an environment where individuals can find hope, healing, and, ultimately, the courage to embrace their journeys.

Through his continued efforts, Crosby is not only reshaping perceptions of addiction and mental health within the sports community but also contributing to a larger societal conversation. He is a testament to the power of resilience, hope, and community support, proving that overcoming adversity and advocating for change is possible. As he continues to share his story and champion the importance of mental health awareness, Maxx Crosby is leaving an indelible mark on the lives of many, inspiring them to seek help, support one another, and embrace the path toward recovery with courage and determination.

Engaging with the Community and Giving Back

Engaging with the community and giving back is vital to personal growth and social responsibility. For Maxx Crosby, this commitment is deeply rooted in his experiences and values. He recognizes that his platform as a professional athlete provides a unique opportunity to create meaningful change in the lives of others. Whether through charity events, mentorship programs, or community outreach initiatives, Crosby consistently seeks ways to connect with those around him, demonstrating that true success goes beyond individual achievements.

Crosby's journey toward becoming an active community member began with a realization that many young people face challenges similar to those he encountered. Growing up, he experienced the pressures of societal expectations and the struggles of self-identity. With this understanding, he has dedicated himself to addressing issues that affect youth in his community, particularly those related to mental health and addiction. By sharing his story and the lessons he has learned, he hopes to inspire others to embrace their struggles and seek help when needed.

One of the most impactful ways Crosby engages with the community is through organized events that promote health and wellness. He often participates in youth sports camps, where he shares his knowledge of the game and encourages young athletes to pursue their dreams. These camps serve as a platform for skill development and a space where young people can learn about teamwork, perseverance, and the importance of maintaining a healthy lifestyle. By fostering an environment of encouragement, Crosby empowers participants to believe in themselves and their potential.

Crosby's philanthropic efforts extend beyond sports. He actively collaborates with organizations focused on mental health and addiction recovery, using his voice to advocate for resources and support systems that can help individuals in need. By partnering with local charities and nonprofits, he amplifies their messages and engages the community in conversations about these critical issues. His presence at fundraising events and awareness campaigns has a tangible impact, attracting attention to causes that often go unnoticed.

Moreover, Crosby recognizes the significance of mentorship in fostering positive change. He has become a mentor for many young athletes, providing guidance and support as they navigate their challenges. Through one-on-one interactions and group sessions, he shares insights from his journey, helping others understand the importance of resilience and hard work. This mentorship goes beyond the field; he encourages mentees to focus on their mental health and well-being, stressing that athletic performance does not define success.

In addition to direct engagement with youth, Crosby has prioritized giving back to his hometown. He understands that staying connected to his roots is essential for personal growth and giving back to the community that shaped him. Organizing events that celebrate local culture and bring together residents, he creates opportunities for individuals to connect and support one another. These gatherings foster a sense of unity and highlight the importance of community support in overcoming adversity.

Another significant aspect of Crosby's engagement is his commitment to education. He often visits schools to speak about the importance of mental health awareness, personal development, and the impact of addiction. By sharing his story in a relatable manner, he captivates young audiences and encourages open dialogue about these topics. This proactive approach helps dismantle mental health stigma, empowering students to prioritize their well-being and seek help when necessary.

Crosby also understands the power of collaboration in driving meaningful change. By teaming up with other athletes and public figures, he amplifies the impact of his advocacy work. Together, they create initiatives that resonate with a broader audience, allowing them to reach individuals who may not otherwise engage with these critical issues. This collaborative spirit fosters a sense of community among athletes, encouraging them to unite for a common cause and use their platforms for good.

Crosby continues to share his journey and the various initiatives he is involved in through social media. He utilizes these platforms to promote his brand and raise awareness about the causes he champions. By sharing stories of resilience, hope, and community support, he inspires others to take action and engage in their communities. His genuine approach fosters connections with fans, motivating them to become involved in local efforts and support one another.

As he moves forward in his career, Crosby remains committed to leaving a lasting impact on the community. He understands that engagement is not a one-time effort but a continuous journey that requires dedication and authenticity. By remaining accessible and involved, he cultivates trust with community members, proving that he genuinely cares about their well-being. This relationship-building is vital for fostering a supportive environment where individuals feel valued and empowered.

Crosby's engagement with the community also emphasizes the importance of listening. He actively seeks feedback from community members, understanding their needs and concerns. This willingness to listen allows him to tailor his efforts in a way that truly resonates with those he aims to help. By centering the voices of community members in his initiatives, he ensures that his advocacy work is relevant and impactful.

Additionally, Crosby recognizes the role of sports in fostering community spirit. He often collaborates with local sports teams and organizations to promote healthy lifestyles and encourage youth participation in athletics. By advocating for accessible sports programs, he believes in the transformative power of physical activity to build confidence and resilience among young people. His passion for sports and community engagement go hand in hand, as he sees firsthand the positive effects of teamwork and camaraderie. Crosby's commitment to giving back is not solely about making a difference but also creating a legacy that inspires future generations. He aspires to be a role model for young athletes, demonstrating that success is not measured solely by accolades but by the impact one has on others. Through his actions, he instills a sense of responsibility in those around him, encouraging them to contribute to their communities and make positive changes.

Crosby embodies the spirit of service and compassion in all of his endeavors. His willingness to share his story, engage with the community, and advocate for important causes exemplifies the essence of leadership. He serves as a reminder that every individual has the power to make a difference, no matter their circumstances. By fostering a culture of support, empathy, and resilience, Crosby contributes to a brighter future for many, leaving an indelible mark on the community he loves.

Maxx Crosby inspires those around him through his engagement and commitment to giving back. His journey is a powerful testament to the impact of community involvement and the importance of lifting others. By prioritizing connection, collaboration, and compassion, he not only enhances his own life but also enriches the lives of countless individuals, forging a path toward a more supportive and inclusive society.

Building a Legacy Beyond Football

Building a legacy transcending football requires a level of dedication, vision, and self-awareness that few athletes possess. Maxx Crosby's journey, both on and off the field, reveals a determination not only to succeed within the game but to leave a lasting impact that extends far beyond the gridiron. His story concerns resilience, personal growth, and a commitment to causes that resonate deeply with him. As he navigates the peaks and valleys of his professional career, Crosby remains focused on constructing a legacy that will endure long after his playing days are over.

From the outset, Crosby's football career was marked by hard work and perseverance. However, it quickly became apparent that his aspirations were not limited to what he could accomplish during a game. He recognized that football was a platform to reach a broader audience and make a real difference in people's lives. The lessons he learned through his challenges, including his struggles with addiction and mental health, helped him see that his story could inspire others for Crosby; building a legacy meant using his platform to share his experiences and encourage those facing similar battles.

At the heart of Crosby's legacy-building efforts is his dedication to raising awareness about mental health and addiction recovery. Having faced these struggles, he understands the importance of openly discussing these topics and reducing their stigma. His candidness about his journey allows others to feel seen and heard, and his willingness to offer support demonstrates his genuine care for those struggling. By making mental health and recovery central to his advocacy, Crosby ensures that his impact will be felt long after his football career has concluded.

One way Crosby extends his legacy beyond football is through mentorship. He actively seeks opportunities to guide and mentor young athletes, providing them with the tools and knowledge to succeed in sports and life. His experiences have taught him that true success comes from overcoming adversity, and he is passionate about helping others understand that setbacks are a natural part of growth. By sharing his wisdom and insights, Crosby helps shape the next generation of athletes, instilling in them the values of perseverance, humility, and compassion.

Crosby's philanthropic efforts are another key component of his legacy. He has consistently shown a deep commitment to giving back to the communities that have supported him throughout his journey. Whether through charity events, fundraising efforts, or simply spending time with those in need, Crosby prioritizes engaging with and uplifting others. His work with organizations focusing on addiction recovery and mental health awareness is particularly meaningful, as it allows him to give back to causes that have personally affected him. By dedicating his time and resources to these initiatives, Crosby ensures that his impact will extend far beyond the football field.

In addition to his philanthropic work, Crosby has shown a keen interest in entrepreneurship and personal development. He understands that building a legacy requires thinking about life after football, and he has taken steps to ensure that he is prepared for whatever comes next. Whether through investments, business ventures, or educational pursuits, Crosby is laying the foundation for a future that will allow him to continue making a difference, even after his playing days are over. His forward-thinking approach demonstrates that he is not content with simply being known as a great football player; he wants to be remembered as someone who used his talents and opportunities to effect meaningful change.

One of the defining aspects of Crosby's legacy is his authenticity. He has remained true to himself throughout his career, never shying away from the challenges he has faced or the mistakes he has made. This honesty has endeared him to fans and peers alike, and it is a critical part of what makes his legacy so impactful. Crosby has created a space for others to do the same by being vulnerable and open about his struggles. His legacy is one of connection, understanding, and empathy, and this genuine approach will ensure his impact endures.

Crosby's leadership qualities have also played a significant role in his efforts to build a legacy beyond football. He is known for his relentless effort and ability to inspire those around him on the field. He carries that same energy into his community work and advocacy efforts off the field. Whether speaking at events, meeting with fans, or working with young athletes, Crosby leads by example, showing that true leadership is about lifting others and creating growth opportunities. His leadership is not about seeking attention or accolades; it is about making a lasting difference in the lives of those around him.

Family and personal relationships have been central to Crosby's journey, and they are also a key part of the legacy he is building. He frequently speaks about the importance of his support system, including his family, friends, and mentors, in helping him overcome his obstacles. By emphasizing the value of these relationships, Crosby reminds others of the importance of surrounding themselves with people who believe in and support them. His legacy is not only about what he accomplishes individually but also his impact on those closest to him. By nurturing these relationships and maintaining a strong sense of community, Crosby sets an example for others to follow.

As Crosby continues to grow personally and professionally, he remains focused on the long-term vision for his life. He understands that building a legacy is an ongoing process requiring continuous effort and reflection. Whether through his advocacy work, mentorship, or philanthropic endeavors, Crosby is always looking for new ways to expand his reach and deepen his impact. His legacy will not be defined by a single moment or achievement but by the accumulation of efforts to improve the world.

Crosby's commitment to building a legacy beyond football is also reflected in his approach to personal growth. He constantly pushes himself to learn and evolve as an athlete and a person. This growth mindset allows him to stay grounded and focused on the bigger picture, even as he navigates the pressures and demands of professional sports. By prioritizing personal development, Crosby ensures that he will continue to have a positive influence long after his playing career ends.

Maxx Crosby's legacy is one of perseverance, compassion, and a desire to leave the world better than he found it. Through his advocacy, mentorship, and community engagement, he proves that success is not just about personal achievements but about how one uses their platform to uplift others. As he continues to build on his legacy, it is clear that Crosby's impact will resonate for years to come, both within the football world and beyond. His story is one of hope and inspiration, reminding us all that no matter the challenges we face, we can create a lasting and meaningful legacy.

Chapter 10: Future Goals and the Path Ahead

Aspirations for an Even Bigger NFL Career

Maxx Crosby's NFL career has already been filled with notable achievements, but his journey is far from complete. His ambitions stretch beyond what he has accomplished thus far, fueled by a desire to elevate his game, leave an indelible mark on the league, and push the boundaries of what's possible for him as an athlete. Crosby's focus is not only on being a dominant force on the field but also on redefining what it means to be a leader in professional sports. His aspirations for an even bigger NFL career speak to a relentless pursuit of growth, excellence, and a legacy that will endure.

Since the Raiders drafted Crosby, he has embodied a work ethic that sets him apart. His rapid rise from being a mid-round draft pick to becoming a cornerstone of the team's defense shows how quickly he adapted to the professional level. However, despite the accolades and recognition, Crosby never seems content to rest on his accomplishments. He views each season as a new opportunity to raise his level of play, and his drive for improvement stems from a personal understanding of what it takes to succeed at the highest level of competition.

One of the key factors that fuels Crosby's ambitions is his understanding of the physical and mental preparation required to sustain a long, impactful NFL career. He knows that the game's physical demands are immense and that maintaining peak performance over many seasons requires constant adaptation and innovation in training. His commitment to refining his body, improving his speed and strength, and staying ahead of his competition has allowed him to consistently perform at a high level. Crosby's offseason work is intense and meticulously planned, ensuring that he's in the best condition to meet the demands of the game.

While physical preparation is crucial, Crosby places equal importance on the mental aspects of the sport. The NFL is a grueling, mentally taxing environment, and athletes are constantly challenged to maintain focus and resilience amid the pressures of competition. For Crosby, part of his aspiration to continue growing as a player is rooted in mastering the mental challenges of being an elite defender. He studies film, analyzes his opponents' tendencies, and works to anticipate plays before they unfold. This mental edge and his natural athleticism help him stay ahead of the game and push his career to new heights.

Crosby's aspirations are also tied to his desire to lead by example. As he matures as a player, his role as a leader within the Raiders' locker room has expanded. He understands leadership isn't just about vocal commands and showing his teammates the commitment and discipline required to succeed. Crosby inspires those around him to elevate their performances by maintaining high standards. His presence on the field is a testament to what hard work can achieve, and his leadership is something he hopes will not only make an impact in his career but also shape the team's culture for years to come.

Another driving force behind Crosby's ambitions is his desire to consistently attend marquee NFL events like the Pro Bowl and All-Pro selections. While these honors acknowledge a player's excellence, Crosby views them as markers of sustained success rather than singular achievements. He aspires to be a perennial contender for these accolades, which would solidify his place among the NFL's elite defenders. More importantly, they would validate the countless hours of preparation and sacrifice that go into being the best. Crosby isn't chasing awards for recognition; he's driven by a need to prove to himself that he can reach the absolute pinnacle of his profession.

At the heart of Crosby's ambitions is his goal of helping the Raiders return to their historic prominence. While individual success is important to him, he understands that team success often defines a player's legacy. Crosby has made it clear that his primary objective is to be a part of a championship-winning team. He envisions leading the Raiders back to Super Bowl contention, restoring the franchise's storied tradition, and bringing a title to Las Vegas. His field contributions and leadership are vital to his vision for his career and the organization's future.

Crosby continues challenging himself to evolve as a player to achieve these goals. He has proven that he can consistently pressure quarterbacks and disrupt offensive plays, but he knows there's always more to learn. One of his ambitions is to become even more versatile, to be a player who can dominate in pass-rushing situations, and be a game-changer in defending the run and covering more ground on the field. This kind of all-around excellence is what Crosby strives for as he seeks to cement his legacy in the league.

Part of what makes Crosby's aspirations so compelling is his humility and understanding that success in the NFL is fleeting. He's well aware that injuries, changes in circumstances, or the unforgiving nature of the sport itself can derail careers. However, rather than allowing these realities to dampen his enthusiasm, Crosby uses them as motivation to maximize every opportunity he gets. He prepares with the knowledge that each season could be a turning point in his career, and he approaches every game as though it's the most important one he'll ever play. This mindset keeps him grounded, focused, and committed to maximizing his talent.

Crosby's ambition isn't solely focused on football, either. He envisions his career as a launching pad for even greater influence off the field, whether through charitable efforts, community engagement, or inspiring the next generation of athletes. His journey, filled with triumphs and challenges, has given him a platform to connect with people meaningfully. Crosby hopes to use his NFL success to broaden his impact, knowing that his role as a professional athlete gives him a unique opportunity to advocate for causes that matter to him, especially around mental health and recovery.

For Crosby, pursuing greatness doesn't stop at personal accolades or career milestones. He sees his career as a chance to continually push the limits of his capabilities, always striving for improvement. Whether mastering new techniques, becoming a more influential leader, or staying at the forefront of innovation in training and preparation, Crosby's mindset is built on the belief that there is always another level to reach. His aspirations for an even bigger NFL career reflect a refusal to be satisfied with what he's already achieved and a constant drive to keep moving forward, even when others might think he has already reached the top.

Maxx Crosby's ambitions are not only about his success but about building something larger, a career that inspires others, lifts his team, and sets a new standard for excellence in the NFL. As he continues to push himself to greater heights, Crosby's determination to forge an even bigger career will undoubtedly impact the league, his teammates, and the broader sports community. His path is relentless growth, unyielding effort, and a clear vision of what lies ahead.

Building on His Personal and Professional Achievements

Maxx Crosby's journey in the NFL is marked not only by his accomplishments on the field but also by his growth as a person and the impact he has made of it. His personal and professional achievements are intertwined, fueling the other, as he strives for excellence in every aspect of his life. For Crosby, success is not defined by any moment or accolade but by the cumulative effect of years of dedication, perseverance, and a commitment to self-improvement. As he moves forward, he remains determined to build on these achievements, constantly pushing himself to set new goals and expand his influence within and beyond the sport.

One of the most striking aspects of Crosby's career is how much he has evolved as a player since entering the league. Drafted as an under-the-radar prospect, he quickly surpassed expectations with his tenacity and work ethic, proving to be one of the league's premier pass rushers. His rise to prominence was no accident. It resulted from countless hours spent honing his craft, improving his technique, and learning from successes and failures. Crosby has never been content with maintaining his level of play; he has always sought to elevate it. Crosby's commitment to becoming a complete player is evident in every game he plays, whether by refining his pass-rush moves or enhancing his physical conditioning.

This drive to continually improve extends far beyond his on-field performance. Crosby's personal life has also been a testament to his growth and resilience. He has openly shared his struggles with addiction, a battle that could have derailed both his career and his life. However, rather than letting these challenges define him, Crosby has used them as a source of strength. His decision to seek help and enter recovery was a turning point for his well-being and his professional career. The discipline and focus required to maintain sobriety have mirrored the work ethic he brings to football, allowing him to channel his energy into becoming a better athlete and a more grounded individual.

Crosby's ability to build on his achievements is rooted in his self-awareness and humility. He recognizes that success, whether on the field or in life, is not guaranteed and must be earned daily. This mindset has allowed him to remain grounded, even as accolades and recognition have poured in. Crosby's humility is reflected in his approach to leadership. As one of the key figures on the Raiders' defense, he understands that his role goes beyond his stats. He takes pride in helping to elevate those around him, whether by setting an example through his work ethic or offering guidance and support to younger teammates. His leadership style is one of action, not words, and his willingness to do whatever it takes for the team has made him a respected figure in the locker room.

The balance between Crosby's personal growth and professional success is perhaps most evident in his role as an advocate for mental health and addiction recovery. Having experienced firsthand the challenges of these issues, Crosby has become a vocal supporter of those facing similar struggles. He has used his platform to speak openly about his journey, helping to destigmatize conversations around mental health and encouraging others to seek help when they need it. This advocacy work has become a significant part of his legacy as he continues to use his influence to make a positive impact on the lives of others.

Crosby's ability to build on his achievements is reflected in his long-term vision for his career. While many athletes may be content with reaching the pinnacle of their sport, Crosby is always looking toward the next challenge. He has set his sights on becoming one of the all-time greats, not just in his statistics but in how he approaches the game. This means continually evolving as a player, adapting to new challenges, and finding ways to remain effective even as the game changes around him. Whether by studying film more intently, working with coaches to develop new techniques, or staying ahead of the curve in terms of training and nutrition, Crosby is always seeking ways to gain an edge.

His desire to build on his professional achievements is closely tied to his sense of responsibility to the Raiders organization and its fans. Crosby understands the weight of wearing the silver and black and has embraced the opportunity to be a key figure in the team's resurgence. He knows his success is only part of the equation; team success ultimately defines a player's legacy. With this in mind, Crosby has committed himself to helping the Raiders return to the top of the NFL, driven by a desire to bring a championship to Las Vegas and solidify the franchise's place in history.

A constant thirst for knowledge and growth characterizes Crosby's approach to building on his personal and professional achievements. He is never satisfied with where he is and is always looking for ways to improve, whether by expanding his skill set or developing new passions. This mentality has led him to explore opportunities outside of football, as he recognizes the importance of preparing for life after the game. Crosby is laying the groundwork for a future as impactful as his football career, whether through business ventures, charitable work, or personal interests.

This broader vision for his life reflects how far Crosby has come since his early days in the league. He has matured into a player who is not only defined by his performance but also by how he carries himself as a leader, a mentor, and a person. His achievements have given him a unique perspective, allowing him to appreciate the bigger picture and understand the importance of using his platform for good. Crosby's growth as an individual has made him more than just an athlete; it has made him a role model within the NFL and beyond.

At the core of Crosby's continued success is his unwavering belief in the power of hard work and resilience. He understands that setbacks are a part of life but doesn't have to define you. This mentality has allowed him to overcome adversity and continue pushing forward, even when the odds have been stacked against him. Whether recovering from an injury, dealing with personal challenges, or facing criticism, Crosby has always found a way to rise above and come back stronger. This resilience is a testament to his character and a key factor in his ability to build on his achievements, no matter the obstacles.

Looking ahead, Crosby's aspirations remain as high as ever. He is not content with his accomplishments; he is focused on what comes next. Whether it's achieving new milestones in his football career, expanding his impact off the field, or continuing to grow as a person, Crosby's journey is far from over. His ability to build on his personal and professional achievements reflects his relentless drive, his commitment to excellence, and his belief that there is always more to achieve, both in football and life. As he continues to push himself to new heights, there is little doubt that Crosby's legacy will only grow.

Cementing His Place Among the NFL Greats

Maxx Crosby's quest to cement his place among the NFL greats is a journey defined by relentless ambition, an insatiable work ethic, and an unwavering belief in his potential. From his early days as an underrated prospect to becoming one of the league's premier defensive players, Crosby has continually defied expectations. Yet, despite the accolades and recognition, he remains focused on achieving more, knowing that greatness is not a destination but an ongoing pursuit.

Crosby's physical gifts are evident; his long frame, explosive speed off the edge, and raw power make him a nightmare for opposing quarterbacks. However, it is his mentality that truly sets him apart. From his rookie season, he displayed an understanding of the game that belied his experience. Unlike some players who rely solely on natural talent, Crosby's success has always resulted from careful preparation and thoughtful execution. He studies film relentlessly, learning the tendencies of offensive linemen, quarterbacks, and entire offensive schemes. This dedication allows him to anticipate plays before they unfold, putting him in a position to disrupt even the most well-designed plays. This attention to detail has elevated him from a promising young player to a cornerstone of the Raiders' defense.

As Crosby's career progresses, it's evident that he draws inspiration from the game's legends, aiming to carve out his legacy alongside the likes of Reggie White, Bruce Smith, and Lawrence Taylor. These names are not simply benchmarks; they represent the level of excellence to which Crosby aspires. To be mentioned in the same breath as these all-time greats requires more than individual accomplishments. It demands a sustained period of dominance, adaptability, and the ability to rise to the occasion in the biggest moments. Crosby is acutely aware of this, and his preparation reflects that understanding.

One of the key attributes that has propelled Crosby toward greatness is his versatility. While he is known for his prowess as a pass rusher, his contributions extend far beyond sacks. He can stop the run, drop into coverage when necessary, and make plays that don't always appear on the stat sheet. It's this all-around ability that makes him indispensable to his team. Greatness in the NFL is often measured by consistency across all aspects of the game, and Crosby's well-rounded skill set has allowed him to be a force every time he steps on the field. Whether the Raiders need a crucial sack or a key tackle on third down, Crosby is always ready to deliver.

Crosby's ascent has not come without obstacles. Like many greats before him, adversity has played a significant role in shaping his career. Injuries, personal battles, and the pressures of performing at an elite level are challenges that every top player faces. What distinguishes Crosby, however, is his resilience in the face of these challenges. Rather than allowing setbacks to derail him, Crosby uses them as motivation. Each obstacle becomes a stepping stone on his path to greatness, a test of his ability to adapt and overcome. This mentality is essential for any player aspiring to reach the game's highest levels.

In addition to his on-field exploits, Crosby understands that legacy is built off the field. The greats of the NFL are remembered not only for their statistics and accolades but for their influence on the game and the people around them. Crosby's leadership has become an integral part of his identity. He leads by example, setting the tone for the Raiders in practice and game day. His work ethic is infectious, and his dedication to his craft inspires those around him. As a captain, Crosby takes pride in holding his teammates accountable and pushing them to reach their full potential. This leadership is critical, as the greats often elevate the players around them, creating a lasting impact beyond their accomplishments.

One of the most telling signs of Crosby's determination to cement his place among the NFL greats is his approach to offseason preparation. While some players may take time off after the grind of a long season, Crosby views the offseason as an opportunity to improve. He consistently pushes himself to get stronger, faster, and more technically sound. His workouts are designed to enhance every aspect of his game, from footwork and hand placement to conditioning and endurance. By attacking the offseason with the same intensity he brings to game day, Crosby ensures he enters each new season better prepared than the last.

Their ability to perform at a high level for an extended period sets the all-time greats apart. Sustained excellence is the true mark of greatness, and Crosby is committed to maintaining his elite status for years. This requires constant evolution. Opposing teams will adapt to his strengths, so Crosby must continuously refine his game to stay ahead. Whether developing new pass-rush moves, studying different offensive schemes, or working with coaches to perfect his technique, Crosby's willingness to evolve will allow him to remain a dominant force in the league.

Moreover, Crosby's mindset is one of continual growth. He doesn't view success as a final destination but as a journey that requires constant effort and improvement. This mentality is shared by many of the game's greatest players, who never stop seeking ways to get better, no matter how much they've already accomplished. Crosby's humility in recognizing that there is always room for improvement is one of the key reasons he is poised to join the ranks of the NFL's elite.

Crosby's pursuit of greatness is not limited to his individual goals. He knows that team success is critical to any player's legacy. Many of the NFL's greatest players are remembered for their accolades and role in leading their teams to championships. Crosby is determined to bring that kind of success to the Raiders. He wants to be remembered as a player who helped restore the franchise to its former glory, delivering championships and creating memories that will last a lifetime for Raiders fans. This commitment to team success is another hallmark of greatness, as the best players understand that their legacy is tied to their team's achievements.

As Crosby continues to build his career, there is little doubt that he is on the path to cementing his place among the NFL greats. His talent, work ethic, leadership, and resilience have already set him apart from many peers. Yet, what truly makes Crosby special is his unrelenting drive to improve. He is never satisfied with past accomplishments and always seeks to improve and push himself to new heights. This mentality is what will ultimately define his legacy. Crosby's journey is far from over, but the foundation he has laid is undeniable. With each passing season, he continues to add to his impressive resume, making his case for a place among the all-time greats. While the future remains unwritten, Crosby's work ethic, talent, and determination ensure that he will leave an indelible mark on the NFL. As he strives for more, both for himself and for his team, Crosby's legacy will only continue to grow, and his place among the NFL's elite will be all but assured.

CONCLUSION

Maxx Crosby's journey in the NFL is far from ordinary. From an under-the-radar prospect to one of the league's most feared and respected defensive players, his rise is a testament to the power of hard work, discipline, and an unyielding belief in self. Crosby embodies the spirit of a player who refuses to be outworked, and his career to date showcases what is possible when talent meets a relentless drive for improvement. He has carved out a path defined by resilience, perseverance, and an unquenchable thirst to achieve greatness, central to his identity both on and off the field.

Crosby's story serves as an inspiration not only to young athletes hoping to make their mark but also to anyone striving to overcome challenges and surpass expectations. From his early years, where he faced limited opportunities and skepticism, to becoming the cornerstone of the Raiders' defense, Crosby never lost sight of his goals. His journey is continuous growth, adapting, learning, and consistently raising his standards. Each season has seen him evolve, not just as a player but as a leader, someone whose presence commands respect and motivates those around him to elevate their game.

Beyond the physical prowess that makes him a formidable opponent, Crosby has demonstrated an intellectual grasp of the sport, elevating his performance to another level. His ability to study the intricacies of his opponents, anticipate their moves, and react with precision has been instrumental in his ascent. But his greatness lies not just in his accomplishments but in his ability to inspire and galvanize his teammates. Leadership, for Crosby, is not about titles or positions. It's about being the hardest worker in the room, setting a standard for excellence, and ensuring that everyone around him rises to meet it.

Off the field, Crosby's story is one of redemption and self-awareness. He has used his platform to shine in the spotlight and

118

shed light on issues that matter deeply to him. His advocacy for mental health and addiction recovery has touched countless lives, showing that being a role model goes far beyond accolades and statistics. His openness about his struggles and his journey to sobriety has given others the courage to confront their challenges, proving that strength isn't just measured by physical achievements, personal growth, and the ability to rise above adversity.

As the years go by, Crosby's legacy is built not just on his statistics or the highlight-reel plays but on his commitment to his team, community, and evolution. His impact on the Raiders has been immeasurable regarding his defensive dominance, the culture of accountability, and the hard work he has helped instill. He is a player who understands that true greatness is not just about excelling for a moment but sustaining that excellence over a career.

Maxx Crosby's future remains bright. With each passing season, his skills sharpen, and his impact deepens. While his story is still being written, the foundation he has laid speaks to a legacy that will endure long after his playing days are over. He is on a path to cement his place among the NFL's elite and inspire future generations of athletes and leaders. Crosby's career will undoubtedly be remembered not only for the sacks and tackles but for the resilience, dedication, and heart that have defined him every step of the way. His legacy will be lasting, built on strength, perseverance, and an unwavering commitment to being the best version of himself both on and off the field.

Made in United States
North Haven, CT
21 October 2024

59281866R00068